THE GOLDEN HAGGADAH

THE GOLDEN HAGGADAH

Bezalel Narkiss

POMEGRANATE ARTBOOKS

In memory of my parents, Mordechai and Nassiah Narkiss

Acknowledgements

The author would like to thank Dr Aliza Cohen-Mushlin and Miss Christine Evans who read my Introduction critically and made it accurate and readable.

The author and publishers would like to thank the copyright holders of illustrations reproduced in this book. All illustrations for which no source is given in the accompanying caption are reproduced by permission of the British Library Board.

Front Cover: Miriam and her maidens play musical instruments. Detail of fol. 15. Fig. 30.

Frontispiece: Pharaoh's daughter and her maidens find Moses. Detail of fol. 9. Fig. 24.

First published 1997 by The British Library
Published in North and South America by
Pomegranate Artbooks, PO Box 6099,
Rohnert Park, California 94927

ISBN 0 87654 481 2

Printed in England

CONTENTS

Introduction *page* 7

The Golden Haggadah 12

The full-page Biblical miniatures 21

The artists of the Biblical miniatures 50

The models for the Biblical miniatures 55

The Jews of Barcelona and the patrons of the Golden Haggadah 64

References 68

Bibliography 70

סדר
הגדה של
פסח
עם שירים מיוחדים, על כל
הנפלאות והנסים, שנעשו
ביצאתם ממצרים
בני חורין
נתנו במתנה הכבודה מרת רויזה
תמ"א בת המפואר כמהר"ר יואב
גאליקן יצ"ו, אל המשכיל
חתנו כמ"ו אליה יצ"ו
בן החכם כמוהר"ר מנחם רבא ישרו
ביום חתונתו וביום שמחת לבו
פה קר"פ
עשירה ימים לחדש חשון הש"ץ שנת גמל

Fig. 1

INTRODUCTION

"*Wherein is this night different from all other nights?*" This is the question which the youngest son of the family traditionally asks his father at the beginning of the Passover Eve ceremony, when the entire family is seated round the table. The father blesses a cup of wine and uncovers the Passover plate or basket, which contains unusual food and three wafers of unleavened bread, thus prompting the son to ask his questions. To encourage the son to ask, the father may even put the basket on the son's head, as can be seen on one of the opening pages of the Barcelona Haggadah in the British Library (fig. 2).[1]

Passover is celebrated annually on the fourteenth day of the month of Nissan, commemorating the Exodus of the Children of Israel from Egypt in the spring month. The term 'Passover' (*Pesaḥ* in Hebrew) is derived from the biblical account of how, during the tenth and last plague in Egypt, the Plague of the Firstborn, God passed over the houses of the Children of Israel and did not kill their firstborn (Exodus 12:21–32). Even before the Plague of the Firstborn, Moses ordered the festival of Passover to be celebrated for seven days

Fig. 1. The title page of the Golden Haggadah, fol. 2, added in 1602 at Carpi by Rabbi Joav Gallico of Asti, on the occasion of the wedding of his daughter Rosa to Rabbi Eliah, son of Menaḥem Rava.

Fig. 2. The father putting the Passover basket on his son's head. Opening miniature of the Barcelona Haggadah of *c.*1340. London, B.L. Add. 14761, fol. 28v.

annually by eating unleavened bread (*maẓah* in Hebrew; Exodus 12:14–20). In their haste to leave Egypt they could not wait for their bread to rise, and so had to bake it unleavened (Exodus 12:39). Moses also ordained the sacrifice of a lamb for the first day of Passover (Exodus 12:5–11, Leviticus 23:12) which, after the building of the Temple in Jerusalem, became the paschal offering already mentioned in the Bible (Deuteronomy 16:1–8). Eating the paschal lamb at a family meal together with *maẓah* (unleavened bread) and *maror* (bitter herbs), as ordained by God through Moses (Exodus 12:8), became the customary beginning of the Passover Eve ritual.

Passover became one of the three pilgrimage festivals of the Temple as early as biblical times (Deuteronomy 16:1–17), the other two being Pentecost and Tabernacles (*Shavu'ot* and *Sukkot* in Hebrew). All three were agricultural harvest festivals in the Land of Israel, concentrated round the bringing of offerings to the Temple in Jerusalem. The paschal lamb had to be offered and eaten in the Temple, 'not at one of the gates of any city' (Deuteronomy 16:5).

During the Second Temple period, while the paschal lamb was being sacrificed on the altar, the Levites recited the 'Egyptian *Hallel*';[2] and eventually it also became customary to recite these psalms during Passover celebrations outside the Temple. Two of the Evangelists mention the reciting of 'hymns' at Christ's Last Supper on Passover Eve (Matthew 26:30, Mark 14:26). These psalms now form part of the Haggadah, preceded by texts and customs added since the destruction of the Temple in 70 AD and the consequent cessation of sacrifices. This event caused the character of Passover to change from an agricultural spring feast to a national festival concerned with the redemption of Israel and the future advent of the Messiah. The story of the oppression in Egypt and of the Exodus became an exemplum for any state of oppression with the hope of future redemption. Thus the Passover ceremony which developed during the first two centuries crystallised into a definite 'order' (*seder* in Hebrew) of texts to be recited and foods to be eaten.

What is a Haggadah?

The Haggadah is a book of ritual for the entire Passover Eve *seder*. It was structured, during the second century, along the lines of a Greek symposium, where philosophical discussion was stimulated by wine, appetising herbs, main courses and desserts (Stein). During the Passover *seder* four obligatory cups of wine are drunk, bitter herbs (*maror*) and unleavened bread (*maẓah*) are eaten, followed by a full meal. The topic of discussion is the Exodus from Egypt and its implications, triggered by Moses' statement: 'And thou shalt *tell thy son* in that day, saying: It is because of that which the Lord did for me, when I came out of Egypt' (Exodus 13:8). The Hebrew term Haggadah means *telling*, and is directly related to the phrase 'tell thy son' in that verse. The Haggadah proper starts, after drinking the first cup of wine and showing the *maẓah*, with four questions, traditionally asked by the youngest son, as to 'Wherein is this night different from all other nights?' The answer to these questions, which is the actual 'telling', namely the Haggadah, is an extensive *midrash* ('exposition' in Hebrew) on some verses from the Bible which give a short historical account of the Exodus from Egypt (Joshua 24:2–4, Deuteronomy 26:5–8).

Although the text of the Haggadah was already fixed in its essentials during the second century AD (Mishnah, *Pesaḥim*, 10), other passages were added later up to the thirteenth century. These are mostly hymns of praise and thanksgiving to God relating to later events in the history of the Jews, laying stress on the similarities between the miraculous delivery from bondage in Egypt and salvation from oppression elsewhere.

Strange as it may seem, Moses, who led the Exodus from Egypt, is not mentioned even once in the Haggadah. This is because of a recension of the text made in the eighth century, during the Karaite controversy in Babylonia. The Karaites rejected rabbinical tradition and the Talmud, basing their teaching solely on the Bible and emphasising the importance of Moses as the sole teacher of Judaism. The *Geonim*, the authoritative rabbis of Babylonia at the time, regarded the Karaites as heretical and ordered the deletion of Moses' name from most ritual texts, including the Haggadah.

As part of the Jewish prayer-book the Haggadah crystallised as a unique entity in the Middle Ages during the period up to the thirteenth century, with slight variations when used in different communities: Middle Eastern, Sephardi (of Spanish origin), Ashkenazi (of Franco-German origin), or Italian. Being a ritual which is celebrated at home, the Haggadah is different from the *Siddur*, the Jewish daily prayer-book, and the *Maḥzor*, the festival prayer-book, both consisting of prayers to be recited mainly in the synagogue. This may have led to the separation of the Haggadah from the general prayer-book and its appearance as a separate book. This happened in the thirteenth century, concurrently with the increase in manuscript production in western Europe in general, when secular workshops for manuscript illumination developed in most important cities, accessible to both lay Christians and Jews. New techniques in the preparation of parchment, inks, colours, gold leaf and other materials brought the acquisition of illuminated manuscripts within the reach of many citizens. Becoming cheaper, an abundance of Hebrew illuminated books were produced in most west European countries and were accessible to more Jewish families, the Haggadah being one of the favourites. As a separate entity, it then became open to the addition of texts and illuminations in accordance with the taste of the patron as well as the ideas of the makers, the scribes and illuminators.

The additions to the text were mostly in the form of prayers and liturgical poems (*piyyutim* in Hebrew) indigenous to the Sephardi or Ashkenazi sphere, as the case may be. Historically, the illuminations may have started as text illustrations when the Haggadah was still part of the general prayer-book, the earliest being the depiction of the *maẓah* and *maror* adjacent to their mention in the text. In a fragment of an eleventh-century Haggadah, probably from Egypt and now in the Budapest Jewish Theological Seminary, there is a picture of a large leaf of *maror*.[3] Later other illustrations were added: some were of a ritual and instructional nature, including the preparations for the Passover Eve feast; others illustrated the story of the Children of Israel in Egypt and of their deliverance from bondage. It would seem that one of the reasons for incorporating illustrations in the Haggadah was to arouse the interest of women and children in the long and tiring verbal ceremony, as the commentator on the Sassoon Haggadah suggested.[4]

By the thirteenth century, when the Haggadah text was fixed and existed as a separate entity, there was no longer any reason to exclude the name of Moses, the leader, from the story of the deliverance from Egypt. However, once his name had been removed from the authorised text of the Haggadah, it could not be replaced, although in the additional material, the *piyyutim* and the illustrations, Moses was given a prominent role.

Illuminating the Haggadah

By the fourteenth century the Haggadah had acquired a relatively fixed decoration programme, which can be divided into four categories. These are the ritual, textual, biblical and eschatological illustrations, all prompted by the text of the Haggadah. They adorned Ashkenazi as well as Sephardi and Italian manuscripts, each community developing its own textual version and its special decoration programme.

The ritual illustrations are mainly instructional in character. They begin with the preparations for Passover: baking the *mazah*, slaughtering the lamb, and cleaning the house. They are followed by scenes showing people coming out of the synagogue, the family seated round the *seder* table, and performing the different rituals of Passover Eve, each according to the customs of their own community.

The textual illustrations do not relate to a ritual, but to something in the text, such as the *mazah* and *maror*, which are mentioned in the saying of Rabban Gamaliel (head of the Sanhedrin in the second century) as quoted in the Mishnah (*Pesaḥim*, 10:5), concerning the three things which have to be recited on Passover Eve (the third being the paschal lamb). Other textual illustrations may portray the different rabbis mentioned in the Haggadah, including Rabban Gamaliel; or perhaps the Four Sons, alluding to the 'Four Ages of Man';[5] an angel pouring out the cup of God's 'wrath upon the Gentiles, who did not recognise Him' (Psalm 79:6); or some sophisticated puns alluding to Hebrew expressions.

Sometimes the Haggadah contained eschatological illustrations relating to the hope of messianic deliverance in the future. One such representation is the Entry of the Righteous into Paradise, evoked by a biblical verse: 'Open for me the gates of the righteous and I will enter them' (Psalm 118: 19). Another eschatological illustration shows the prophet Elijah riding a donkey, personifying the harbinger of the Messiah. According to the Jewish tradition, Elijah appears on every Passover Eve, when the door is customarily opened for him immediately after the main meal, at the beginning of the second part of the *seder*, when the verse 'Pour out Thy wrath upon the Gentiles, who did not recognise Thee'(Psalm 129:6) is recited.

The most interesting category of Haggadah illustrations are the biblical pictures. Sometimes they are placed near the texts of the biblical and midrashic episodes related to the story of the Exodus, preceded by the history of the patriarchs. The cycle of illustrations was sometimes broadened to include other episodes from the Creation of the World to the death of Moses and beyond, up to the lives of the prophets. Some of the biblical episodes are confused with the ritual pictures: for example, the historical baking of the *mazah* and smearing the lintel with the blood of the lamb were confused with the preparations for the Passover contemporary with the medieval manuscript. Many of the historical illustrations are not purely biblical, but also contain imagery from the legendary expositions of the Jewish *midrash*. Some of this legendary material was based on early rabbinical exegesis in the Mishnah, the *Talmud* or in the Aramaic translations (*Targum* in Hebrew); other material is extracted from later medieval *midrashim*. The most commonly illustrated midrashic stories in the different Haggadah manuscripts are the episodes of Abraham cast into the fire to be tested by King Nimrod; Joseph meeting an angel on the way to meet his brothers in Dothan; and the testing of the baby Moses by means of gold and live coal. Some of these legendary episodes and many others are depicted in the Golden Haggadah, as can be seen below.

The Ashkenazi, Sephardi and Italian Haggadoth

Three main types of medieval illuminated Haggadoth can be distinguished on the basis of their decoration programme and place of origin: Ashkenazi, Sephardi, and Italian.

The Ashkenazi Haggadoth from northern France and Germany are decorated with illustrations in the margins surrounding the text, rather like the illuminated monastic psalters in Byzantium, and consist of two essential groups. The earlier group places the ritual and biblical illustrations next to the relevant text, the earliest example of this being the Birds' Heads Haggadah of about 1300.[6] The later group contains a cycle of pictures from any book of the Bible, depicted chronologically, and placed with no direct relation to the text of the Haggadah, for example the Yahudah Haggadah of the early fifteenth century[7] and its twin the Second Nuremberg Haggadah.[8]

The Sephardi type, from Spain and southern France, usually has fewer illustrations in the text, and those mainly ritual, but also biblical and textual, such as the Barcelona Haggadah in the British Library.[9] The more sumptuous codices have a series of full-page miniatures, mostly from Genesis and Exodus, but also from other books of the Bible. These full-page miniatures usually precede the Haggadah text, occupying separate quires, rather like the west European psalter manuscripts of the thirteenth and fourteenth centuries. One of the earliest and most sumptuous Sephardi Haggadoth is the Golden Haggadah.[10] The Sarajevo Haggadah of the late fourteenth century has the richest range of biblical illustrations, starting with the creation of the world and ending with Moses blessing Israel.[11]

The third type, the Italian, may have been based historically on Middle Eastern illuminations in the prayer-book, although none has survived. The early Italian illuminated Haggadah may thus have been the earliest of the three types in Europe, and the model for the others. In the fifteenth century the Italian Haggadoth were mainly influenced by the Ashkenazi type, containing marginal illustrations only. Following an influx of Jews expelled from Germany, a new group of Italo-Ashkenazi Haggadoth emerged, copied in Ashkenazi script and with the Ashkenazi decoration programme, but illuminated in the Italian style. The best examples of this group are the Haggadoth copied and illuminated by Joel ben Simeon of Bonn, who pursued his career in Lombardy, such as the Washington Haggadah of 1478.[12]

Not every Jewish household during the late Middle Ages could afford to own an illuminated Haggadah. It was mainly the wealthier Jews, merchants and money-lenders in Germany and Italy, or courtiers serving the kings and princes of Spain, Majorca and southern France in particular as secular and financial administrators, who had the knowledge and could afford such manuscripts. The secular and religious culture of their Christian masters formed the taste of these Jewish courtiers, and it pleased them to commission similar illuminated manuscripts. Testimony to that effect can be found in the introduction to the Book *Ma'aseh Efod* by Rabbi Profiat Duran of Majorca (1361–1444), who fled to Algiers during the Disturbances of 1391 and completed his book there in 1403: 'The sixth rule is that study should be in beautiful and pleasing books, written in harmonious script, on fine vellum with luxurious bindings, and in pleasant buildings . . . since looking at and studying beautiful forms with delicate drawings and fine paintings is one of the things which pleases the soul, encourages and strengthens its powers. It has been one of the virtues of our nation that the rich and important in every generation have always exerted an effort to produce beautiful codices.'

THE GOLDEN HAGGADAH

The Manuscript

Of seventeen Spanish illuminated manuscripts of the Passover Haggadah, the Golden Haggadah is undoubtedly the most sumptuous and one of the oldest, originating from Barcelona around 1320.[13] It is a medium-sized codex measuring 247 × 195mm (9.7 × 7.7 inches), comprising 102 folios, 100 of which are of vellum. The first and last folios are paper fly-leaves, which are part of the seventeenth-century, blind-tooled leather binding of delicately decorated brown morocco. As in other sumptuous Spanish illuminated Haggadah manuscripts, the contents of the Golden Haggadah form three main parts:

(1) Full-page miniatures; (2) The text of the Haggadah; (3) Liturgical poems and prayers for Passover.

(1) Full-page miniatures on alternate folios 2v–15 contain representations of the biblical story of Genesis and Exodus, which will be dealt with extensively below.

(2) The text of the Haggadah on folios 24v–55v, according to the Sephardi rite and customs.[14] These include a benediction over the washing of hands after drinking the first cup of wine, which is not recited in the other rites; and references to the custom of using a basket rather than the Ashkenazi plate to hold the symbolic food on the *seder* table. It also includes some special Sephardi variations of the text, such as the opening phrase 'When coming from the synagogue', which does not appear in Ashkenazi Haggadoth; and a variant for reciting 'This bread of affliction' (*Ha laḥma anya* in Aramaic). It has only one verse for *Shefokh* ('Pour out Thy wrath'), and a short version of the *Hallel*, without the augmented section of *Nishmat* ('The breath of all beings').

(3) A collection of liturgical poems (*piyyutim* in Hebrew) of Sephardi rite,[15] divided into two sections: the first, for Passover Eve, preceding the Haggadah text (on fols. 16v–23v); and the second section following the text of the Haggadah. In the latter the *piyyutim* are mixed with biblical and mishnaic readings for the entire week of Passover (on fols. 56v–101v). These also include some special Sephardi *piyyutim*.[16]

Each of these three parts of the Golden Haggadah may have been executed in a different workshop. Although all three parts are the same size and are bound together in one volume measuring 247 × 195mm (9.7 × 7.7 inches), and most of the thirteen quires, as in most Sephardi manuscripts of the period, consist of eight leaves each, there are minor differences in other respects. For example, the thickness of the parchment differs in each part; and the two parts of the text differ slightly in the type of script, ink, number of lines per page, and in particular in the spaces allotted for text and miniatures.

The actual text of the Haggadah in quires IV–VII is written on both sides of well chalked, thick, mature vellum. The Sephardi script of large bold square letters is written in dark brown ink, ten lines to a page. The text space in these quires measures 170 × 130mm (6.6 × 5.1 inches). Each page is boldly ruled with a stylus on the hair side with two vertical marginal lines and ten horizontal lines from which the letters are suspended.

The seven quires containing the *piyyutim* (III, VIII–XIII) are written in a small, delicate square Sephardi script in twenty-six lines and two columns per page, in light brown ink, on both sides of the leaf. The vellum is soft and of medium thickness, well chalked on the flesh side only. The text space measures 158 × 130mm (6.2 × 5.1 inches). Two marginal lines are ruled with a stylus on each page and twenty-six horizontal lines across each bifolium. There are also some differences between the letters used in the Haggadah and the *piyyutim*, which may support an assumption that they were written by two scribes.[17]

The first two quires with the full-page miniatures, painted only on the flesh side of the vellum, are from a mature animal but not of equal thickness: the first quire is of medium thickness, the second much thicker. They were originally composed of eight leaves each, but since the last two leaves of the second quire were cut out, the binder attached the first leaf of the second quire to the first quire, which now contains nine instead of eight leaves.

There are also differences in the size of the miniatures in each original quire. Those of the original quire I (fols. 2–9) measure 178 × 156mm (7 × 6.1 inches), whereas those of the original quire II (fols. 10–15) measure 180 × 152mm (7.1 × 6 inches).

It will be shown below that each original quire was painted by a different artist.

History

In 1864, after the death of the Paduan collector Giuseppe Almanzi, his friend Rabbi Samuel David Luzzatto, a major figure in Italian-Jewish scholarship, published an extensive catalogue of Almanzi's Hebrew manuscript collection.[18] According to the *Catalogue*, the entire collection was due to be sold in one lot 'except for manuscript 328 (the Haggadah on vellum, ornamented with many miniatures and decorations), which will be sold separately', since it was considered so valuable. In spite of this note, the entire Almanzi Collection, including the Haggadah, was purchased by the British Museum on 14 October 1865 for the mere sum of £1,000.[19] It is not known how and when the Haggadah came into the possession of Giuseppe Almanzi, who was a merchant, a poet and an avid manuscript collector. It must have reached Italy around 1492, when many Jewish families, expelled from Spain, came to Italy.

The earliest known owner of the manuscript was Rabbi Joav Gallico of Asti in the Duchy of Savoy, known as the compiler of an alphabetical Talmudic lexicon in Asti, before he moved to Governolo in 1582, where he was a judge. On 12 October 1602 he became the rabbi of the Jewish community in Mantua, and on 25 October that same year he was in Carpi, near Modena, celebrating the wedding of his daughter, 'the noble Rosa', when he gave the Haggadah to 'his learned son-in-law Eliah, son of Menaḥem Rava'.

Like Joav Gallico, both Eliah and his father, Menaḥem Rava, were rabbinic scholars, fairly well known in northern Italy in their time, and were regarded as members of the intelligentsia of the Jewish communities.[20] The elaborate title page, which Rabbi Joav Gallico added on the formerly blank folio 2 of the Haggadah (fig. 1), is modelled after formal title pages in printed books of the time. The heavy portal is flanked by two caryatid mermaids carrying the arched pediment with a winged face in its centre. The inscription withịn the arched opening states the fact of the wedding gift, and gives the place and date of the occasion.

Rabbi Gallico also commissioned the joint armorial device of both families on another originally blank folio, 16 (fig. 3). The oval device is bisected vertically. On the right are the Gallico arms of a cock *vigilant* facing a stalk of corn, with a crescent and a six-pointed star in the sky above. On the left is the Rava device, with a crouching lion *gardant* in front of a mountain cave, and an eight-pointed star in the sky above. The motto, taken from Jacob's blessing of his son Judah (Genesis 49:9), 'He stooped down, he crouched as a lion; and as an old lion, who shall rouse him up?' is written in a banderole above the device. The motto and the device of a lion may point to a tradition that ascribed the Rava family to the Tribe of Judah. The device is supported by two naked mermaids in profile, with a plinth and crest of metallic-looking scrolls, and a face in the middle of the crest.

The other originally blank folios (3v–4, 5v–6, 7v–8, 9v–10, 11v–12 and 13v–14) contain a rhymed poem, possibly by Rabbi Joav Gallico himself, consisting of 54 rules and customs for Passover. The last folio (15v) contains a cabbalistic interpretation of the common Signs of the Passover *Seder: Qadesh ū-Reḥaẓ* ('pronounce the *benediction* over wine *and wash* your hands'). All these folios are framed by a gold band surrounded by dense ochre leaves.

Rabbi Joav Gallico may have purchased the Haggadah in Carpi not long before the wedding, since it is plausible that the manuscript was in Carpi as early as February 1599, when it was signed on the last page of the manuscript (folio 101v) by the censor: *Fra Luigi da*

Fig. 3. Armorial device of the Gallico and Rava families, added at Carpi in 1602 on the occasion of the wedding of Eliah Rava and Rosa Gallico. The Golden Haggadah, fol. 16.

Bologna. In 1597 Luigi da Bologna, a Jewish convert to Christianity and a Dominican monk, became an expurgator of Hebrew books in the district of Modena in the Duchy of the House of Este, working mainly in Carpi. Luigi's statement that he revised the book in February 1599 is supported by his signature in other books and manuscripts in Carpi in 1599.[21] However, other censors had to expurgate the Haggadah again, possibly because the Pope did not trust Luigi's work. These were Camillo Jaghel in 1613 and Renato da Modena in 1626, both signing their names on the same last page.[22]

Strange as it may seem, two years after the Haggadah was given to 'the noble Rosa' and 'the learned Eliah Rava', it passed by legacy to 'the young Arieh on 28 November 1604, who inherited this together with his brothers', as he wrote in the top left-hand corner of the title page. Since Eliah Rava was still alive in 1605, when he published his father's book *Beit Mo'ed* in Venice, it may be assumed that the young couple soon sold their valuable gift to someone who died in 1604 and left the Haggadah to his sons as part of their legacy. On the paper fly-leaf (fol. 1) there is a record of the circumcision of a son, Azariah Ẓidkiah Ḥayim, on 22 January 1689, probably still in Modena.

If the manuscript remained in the Modena-Mantua region at the end of the seventeenth century, it was used in poorer circumstances at Passover in the newly instituted ghettoes forced on the Jews in this region. The economic situation in Modena deteriorated still further in the second half of the eighteenth century. However, with its incorporation into the Cisalpine Republic in 1792, the restrictions upon the Jews were officially abolished, and reform and enlightenment brought more freedom into Jewish life, so that the Golden Haggadah may have been housed in conditions better befitting its status as the finest surviving Sephardi illuminated Haggadah.

There is no evidence indicating when Giuseppe Almanzi acquired the Haggadah, although this was probably by the middle of the nineteenth century.

The Text Illumination of the Golden Haggadah

The Golden Haggadah itself has only two large text illustrations, those of the *maẓah* and the *maror*, and possibly another small one of drinking wine. Otherwise the text decorations of the Haggadah and the *piyyutim* consist mostly of coloured initial words as headings for the different paragraphs, and marginal extensions.

The round wafer of the *maẓah* on folio 44v (fig. 4) is decorated with a colourful geometric interlace resembling Moslem arabesque patterns, which existed in Europe wherever Moslem culture flourished, such as Spain and Sicily. Similar arabesque patterns also appear in an initial-word panel in the *piyyutim* (fol. 78v, fig. 5), as well as on objects in the full-page miniatures of the Haggadah, such as Jacob's pillow (fol. 8v) and Miriam's square tambourine (fol. 15, fig. 30). These survivals of Islamic patterns in Gothic Hebrew manuscripts may be further pointers to the likely existence of earlier Hebrew illuminated manuscripts in Moslem Spain, none of which has survived.

Large full-page decorated *maẓoth*, which appear in most illuminated Sephardi Haggadoth, may reflect a tradition of decorated *maẓoth* in Haggadoth and prayer-books from Moslem Spain, and earlier from the Middle East. There is evidence of decorated *maẓoth* existing from the time of the Second Temple. In the Talmud there is a controversy over the 'painted *mazoth*' (*srikin ha-mezuyarin* in Aramaic), where they were prohibited because of the fear that images might be created on them.[23] It would seem that the 'painting' was done by impressing the wafer with a punch, which prevented the dough from rising. The question was still debated in the fourteenth century, as evidenced by a statement by the anonymous commentator on the laws of Passover in the Sassoon Haggadah.[24] He explains that the prohibition of *srikin mezuyarin* is obsolete, 'since now that our custom of painting them has spread, anybody can do it... with a wide comb. We should only be careful not to tarry over the dough, lest it rise... and I have heard that punching the *mazah* was a custom of the "ancients"... since punching prevents the dough from rising.' It could, indeed, have been a tradition to decorate the *mazah* since the time of the Second Temple, and those depicted in the Spanish Haggadoth may have been a contemporary rendering of the former. Some of these *mazoth* are very elaborate in their decoration: the *mazah* in the Barcelona Haggadah in the British Library (fig. 6)[25] represents the Harmony of the Universe, with the four winds blowing at its corners and five musicians sounding the harmony (Ameisenowa). Other Spanish Haggadoth have a large *mazah* supported by two men.

The *maror* in many Sephardi Haggadoth is also supported by two men, though in the Golden Haggadah it stands by itself, in a full page on folio 45v (fig. 7), as a bunch of green lettuce leaves kept together by a decorated holder.

There may be one other text illustration in the Golden Haggadah. On folio 27 (fig. 8) a dragon is lying on top of the initial-word panel for the benediction of the first cup of wine. The grotesque dragon is drinking from a long-necked jar and holding another similar jar in its other hand.

Fig. 4

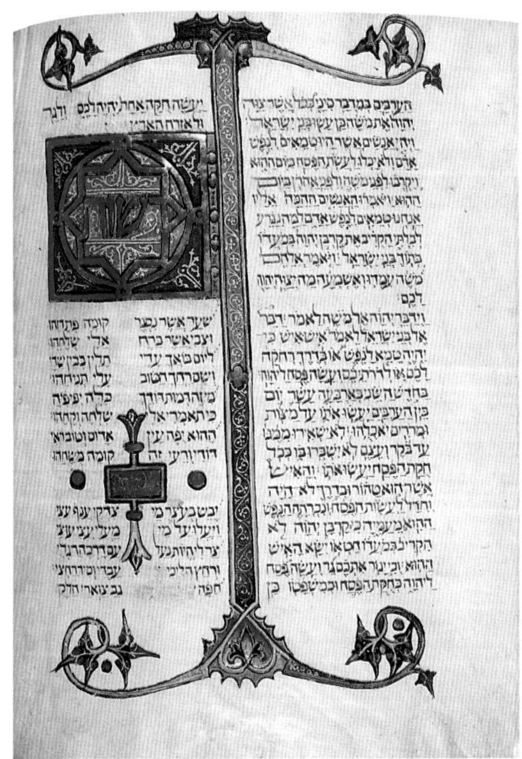

Fig. 5

Fig. 6

Fig. 7

Fig. 8

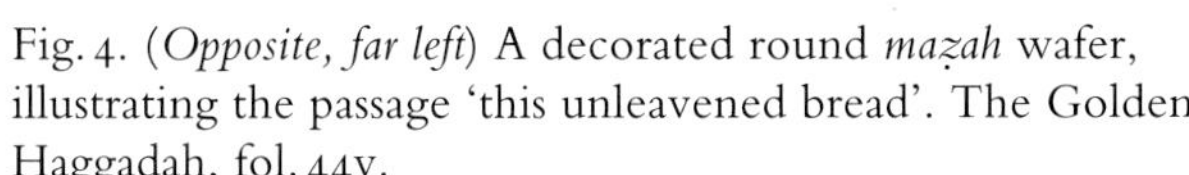

Fig. 4. (*Opposite, far left*) A decorated round *mazah* wafer, illustrating the passage 'this unleavened bread'. The Golden Haggadah, fol. 44v.

Fig. 5. (*Opposite, left*) A decorative panel and foliate scrolls at the opening of the *piyyutim* for the seventh day of Passover week. The Golden Haggadah, fol. 78v.

Fig. 6. (*Above, left*) The *mazah* as the Harmony of the Universe, with putti blowing trumpets representing the four winds, and musicians sounding the harmony. The Barcelona Haggadah, *c.* 1340. London, B.L. Add. 14761, fol. 61.

Fig. 7. (*Above, right*) Lettuce leaves, illustrating the passage 'this bitter herb'. The Golden Haggadah, fol. 45v.

Fig. 8. (*Right*) A dragon drinking wine from a jar, illustrating the initial word 'and drinking' of the benediction for the first cup of wine drunk on Passover Eve. The Golden Haggadah, fol. 27. (Detail).

Fig. 9. (*Above*) A dog with a gold ball. A decorative grotesque at the opening of the Golden Haggadah, fol. 16v. (Detail).

Fig. 10. (*Right*) Decorated ascenders extending from an initial-word panel, foliate frame, and a hybrid playing a bagpipe. The Golden Haggadah, fol. 22v. (Detail).

Other traditional decorative elements from Sephardi Haggadoth are found in the Golden Haggadah. Most of them are common Gothic manuscript illuminations of panels with marginal extensions. Stylistically those in the Golden Haggadah are related to undulating foliate scrolls of the end of the thirteenth century from northern France. These are more fleshy, and have grotesques and hybrids attached to the scrolls, such as a dog with a gold ball (fol. 16v, fig. 9), or a hybrid playing a bagpipe (fol. 22v, fig. 10). Usually the scrolls extend from initial-word panels, not from an initial-letter panel as in Latin manuscripts. This feature developed in Hebrew manuscripts in the early Middle Ages in the Middle East, since Hebrew, like Arabic, has no capital letters. The initial words in the Golden Haggadah are mostly written in large letters in colours, gold or silver, usually framed to create a panel painted in different colours, although some panels are filled with filigree pen decoration, as on folios 16v (fig. 9), 27 (fig. 8), 41v (fig. 11), 44v (fig. 4), 55v (fig. 12), 56v (fig. 13), and 78v (fig. 5). Some of the initial words in the Golden Haggadah are composed of zoomorphic letters, such as those on folios 31v (fig. 14) and 33v. This kind of letter is known to have been used in Merovingian illuminated manuscripts of the seventh and eighth centuries, as well as in Armenian illumination from the Middle East of the twelfth and thirteenth centuries. The

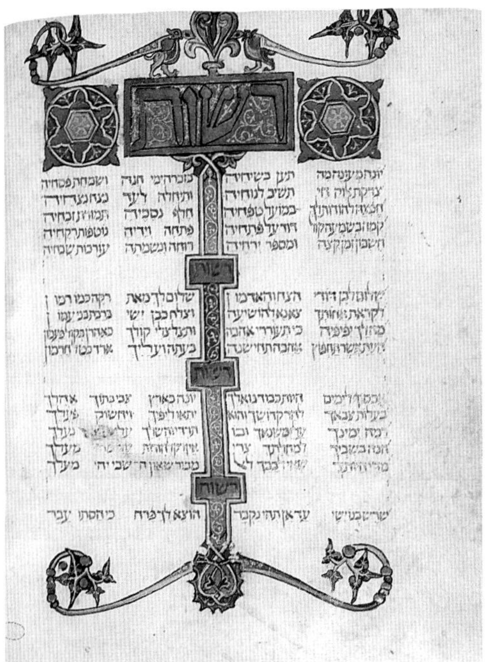

Fig. 11. (*Top left*) The words *Ilu* and *Velo* repeated to create two side panels flanking the text column of the poem *Dayyenu*. The Golden Haggadah, fol. 41v.

Fig. 12. (*Top right*) A descender from the last initial-word panel of the text of the Golden Haggadah, fol. 55v.

Fig. 13. (*Bottom left*) A decorative row of initial-word panels for *piyyutim* at the beginning of Passover week. The Golden Haggadah, fol. 56v.

Fig. 14. (*Bottom right*) An initial word composed of zoomorphic letters. The Golden Haggadah, fol. 31v.

Fig. 15. (*Above, left*) A descender and ascenders extending from the initial-word panels of the text recited after the meal, 'Pour out thy wrath'. The Golden Haggadah, fol. 50.

Fig. 16. (*Above, right*) Three letters *yod*, a contraction of the name of God, within a lotus bud motif. The Golden Haggadah, fol. 51.

Middle Eastern origin of zoomorphic letters may be supported by the fact that medieval Islamic bronze vessels had similar letters inlaid in silver. The Hamilton *Siddur*, also from Spain *c.*1300, which includes a Haggadah, is decorated with similar zoomorphic and anthropocephalic letters.[26] The illuminator of the Sephardi Bible from Cervera of 1300 painted his name in similar letters.[27]

The illuminator of the Golden Haggadah used other traditional motifs to decorate the text, for example the prolongations of letters which naturally have long 'legs' or 'flags' in the Hebrew alphabet, as on folios 32v, 43v, 47 and 50 (fig. 15). Using letters as a means of decoration is also a common feature in Hebrew and Arabic manuscripts. One of the most traditional decorations in the Haggadah is the use of repeated words of a prayer or *piyyut* to build a column of script on either side of the page, as in the poem *Dayyenu* on folio 41v (fig. 11). This motif of repeated words in *Dayyenu* is known from the eleventh century on in Egypt, for example in a fragment of a Haggadah from the Fustat Genizah.[28] Another such device is the three letters *yod* – the abbreviated name of God – forming a panel in the shape of a lotus bud, a common Persian motif (folio 51, fig. 16).

Although the style of decoration of the Golden Haggadah is contemporary, many of the motifs are of traditional Middle Eastern origin.

THE FULL-PAGE BIBLICAL MINIATURES

The well deserved fame of the illuminated Sephardi *Haggadoth* depends on the full-page miniatures attached to the richest of them. These depict a chronological sequence of biblical episodes, most of which are derived from the book of Exodus, some with additional episodes from Genesis, and a few from other books of the Bible. At the end of the biblical sequence of miniatures there usually follows a short cycle of liturgical scenes illustrating the preparations for the Passover Eve ceremony.

The fourteen full-page miniatures of the Golden Haggadah are each divided into four panels, about 80 × 70mm (3.1 × 2.8 inches), some of which depict more than one episode. Thus a cycle of seventy-one episodes from Genesis and Exodus is arranged in fifty-three panels, beginning with Adam naming the animals and ending with Miriam playing and singing after the Passage of the Red Sea (Exodus 15:20). Three additional panels, depicting five ritual scenes, follow. The name 'Golden Haggadah' was given to the manuscript because of the gold-leaf ground of the biblical miniatures richly illuminating each page.

The miniatures are painted on the flesh side of the skin, beginning on the verso of folio 2 and extending to the recto of folio 15. The original arrangement was of pairs of miniature pages facing each other, followed by pairs of blank pages; but in the seventeenth century the blank pages were filled with a frontispiece, an armorial device, and twelve pages of a Passover poem with a decorated foliate frame.

Each panel is framed by blue or brown bands decorated with white rinceaux, pen scrolls or zigzag patterns, and bordered by vermilion or green fillets. Small gold squares are stamped in the corners of each panel. Folios 2, 9–15 have additional foliate pen scrolls extending from the corners. The panels have a stamped diapered pattern with studs on a burnished gold-leaf background. The shapes of the figures, objects and landscapes are outlined in black and painted in several shades of blue, wine red, vermilion, olive green, grey, violet-grey, pink, magenta, brown and dusky gold, all heightened with lighter shades. The landscape consists of step-like rock shapes in brown and violet-grey, with some tufts of dark green grass and flowers. Water is depicted by wavy stripes of two shades of blue. Trees have violet-grey trunks, round tops of dark bottle green, and leaves outlined in black, with some white flowers. Segments of sky are in violet-grey.

Buildings, with doors, windows and dome-like interiors, in green, brown, magenta and blue, are seen mainly from the exterior: many look like domed baldachins; two have coffered ceilings (fol. 15). Domatomorphic furniture is in colours similar to the buildings.

The human figures, proportionally balanced but large compared to the landscape and other objects, are Gothic in style and expressive in movement and gesture. Faces and bare skin are white, heightened with pink; facial features are in black. Clothes, curtains, sheets and table-cloths are draped in soft folds, with shadows and highlights in different shades of the same colour and black and white lines. Where groups of people appear, only those in front are shown in full; of the rest, parts of heads, or even only one eye (scene 18) are shown. Animals are in their natural colours; sheep are white with linear wool.

NOTE

The sequence of episodes and compartments is usually from right to left, and from top (a = right and b = left) to bottom (c = right and d = left).

The captions to the panels, written in a small square script, are probably contemporary with those in the Haggadah and the *piyyutim*, although they were written by another hand. In most cases they are paraphrases of biblical verses that describe the episodes correctly; they are therefore cited in the descriptions as titles (in inverted commas).

1. *Biblical Scenes*

fol. 2v, a (1) 'Adam gives names to the beasts and the cattle' (based on Genesis 2:19–20). To the left, Adam is seated on the ground, naked, pointing with his left hand to the birds on top of a tree in the middle of the compartment, and with his right hand to the animals approaching him from the right. Among the animals are a reptile, a goat nibbling at a second tree, two sheep, a red bull, two donkeys and a rabbit.

fol. 2v, b, right (2) The creation of Eve (Genesis 2:21–22). Eve's naked bust emerges from Adam's right side as he lies naked on the ground asleep.

fol. 2v, b, left (3) The temptation (Genesis 3:1–8). On either side of the Tree of Knowledge, round which the serpent is coiled, are Adam and Eve, covering their nakedness with fig leaves. From a segment of sky in the top right-hand corner a winged angel is pointing at them. Inscribed 'Adam and his wife naked.'

fol. 2v, c, right (4) 'Cain and Abel offer a sacrifice' (based on Genesis 4:3–5). Abel, carrying a lamb in his covered hands, is standing to the right of a columnar altar with a fire on top. The flame is bending towards Cain, who is standing on the left holding a sheaf of corn in his bare hands and looking away from the altar.

fol. 2v, c, left (5) 'And Cain rose up [against Abel his brother and slew him]' (Genesis 4:8). Cain holds a long-handled axe in his left hand and looks up at the winged angel, who is emerging from a segment of sky to reproach him. Under Cain's feet and partly buried in the ground are Abel's bloody head and arm (Genesis 4:9–10). The human figures are damaged.

fol. 2v, d (6) 'Noah and his wife and his sons come out of the ark' (based on Genesis 8:18–19). In the middle, a bearded Noah helps two sheep to come out of the arched door of a box-like ark. Behind him are his wife and four children. In front of him are the animals: two more sheep, a donkey, a red bull and a goat; below him is a pig. On top of the left-hand side of the ark is a dove holding a branch in its beak.

אדם קורא שמות לחיות ולבהמות
אדם ואשתו ערומים
נח ואשתו ובניו יוצאים מן התיבה

Fig. 17

Fig. 18

fol. 3r, a, right (7) 'And he planted a vineyard' (Genesis 9:20). Noah, wearing a white apron, is cutting the red clusters of grapes with a knife. A basket full of red grapes is near him (not recorded in the Bible).

fol. 3r, a, left (8) 'And he drank of the wine, and was drunken; and he was uncovered' (Genesis 9:21). Noah is lying naked on the ground, asleep. Behind him are two youths, Shem and Japheth, holding a blue and vermilion cloth to cover Noah. Inscribed 'And their faces were backward' (Genesis 9:23).

fol. 3r, b (9) The builders of the Tower of Babel kill each other (Genesis 11:1–9; based on *Genesis Rabbah* 38:10). To the right at the bottom of a white stone tower is a man stabbing in the back another who is drawing up a bucket with a pulley. Below, a man mixing mortar with a hoe is being stoned by another who is leaning out of a low window in the tower. In front of the tower two men are stabbing each other. The architect, standing on the left in a long green robe, is being stoned by a man from a higher window. On top of the tower is a man stabbing another in the back. Inscribed 'The divided generation', the mishnaic term for this episode (Mishnah *Bava Meẓia* 4:2; *Sanhedrin* 10:3, based on Genesis 10:25).

fol. 3r, c (10) 'Nimrod and his wise men throw Abraham into the fiery furnace' (based on *Genesis Rabbah* 38:13; Babylonian Talmud, *Pesaḥim* 118a; *Tana De-ve: Eliyahu* 6). To the right is the crowned Nimrod, seated under a green canopy, pointing at Abraham, who is being thrown by two attendants into the hands of two winged angels who appear from the fire in a barrel-like furnace in the left-hand corner. Below the king sit two of his counsellors.

fol. 3r, d (11) Abraham's hospitality and the prophecy to Sarah. Inscribed '[And he] stands by them [under the tree and they did eat]' (Genesis 18:8). Three winged angels, sitting under a tree behind a set table, point to Abraham on the left, who is waiting on them holding a flask and pointing to Sarah, who stands within an open edifice. Inscribed '[And he said:] Behold, in the tent' (Genesis 18:9).

fol. 4v, a (12) 'Lot and his daughters flee'. To the right is Lot, pushing four children in front of him. In the middle, on top of a stepped rock, is the white figure of Lot's wife, inscribed 'And she became a pillar of salt' (Genesis 19:26). To the left are four bleeding heads among the ruins of collapsed houses and parts of walls. Inscribed 'The overthrow of Sodom'.

fol. 4v, b, right (13) The binding of Isaac, inscribed 'Abide ye here with the ass' (Genesis 22:5). Abraham's two young attendants are standing behind the ass.

fol. 4v, b, left (14) 'And he bound Isaac his son' (Genesis 22:9). Isaac is lying on the ground with hands bound. Kneeling over him is Abraham, holding a knife and looking backwards at a winged angel, who is appearing from a segment of sky and pointing to a ram that is hanging vertically from a tree in the middle of the panel. Inscribed 'And behold, a ram' (Genesis 22:13).

fol. 4v, c, left (15) Isaac blessing Jacob. Inscribed 'Come near, I pray thee, that I may feel thee' (Genesis 27:21). Isaac, sitting on the left behind a table laid with a lamb on a plate, is touching Jacob's hands and neck. Behind Jacob is Rebecca.

fol. 4v, c, right (16) 'And Esau [his brother came in from his hunting]' (Genesis 27:30). Esau is approaching from the right, carrying a hare hanging from a club over his shoulder and armed with a bow and arrows.

The two scenes in this compartment (15–16) should be read from left to right, as described above. A large green building serves as background for both.

fol. 4v, d (17) Jacob's dream. Inscribed 'A ladder set up on earth ... the angels of God ascending and descending' (Genesis 28:12). To the left is 'Jacob', lying on the ground asleep. One angel is ascending the ladder, which is placed diagonally, and another is descending it. The head and wing of another angel appear from a rectangular aperture in the segment of sky in the top right-hand corner. Two other angels are walking on the ground, one touching Jacob's head.

לוט ובנותיו בורחים
ותהי נציב מלח
הפיכת סדום
שבו לכם פה עם החמור
והנה איל
ויעקד את יצחק בנו

Fig. 19

5
ויאבק איש עמו
ויעבר את מעבר יבק
חלומות יוסף
אחי יוסף
ויגער בו אביו
וימצאהו איש

Fig. 20

fol. 5r, a, left (18) 'And he passed over the ford Jabbok' (Genesis 32:22–23). Jacob and seven other people are walking on the left side of the Jabbok, painted diagonally from about the middle of the panel to the bottom left-hand corner.

fol. 5r, a, right (19) Jacob wrestling with the angel. Inscribed 'And a man wrestled with him' (Genesis 32:24–25).

Scenes 18–19 should be read from left to right, as described above.

fol. 5r, b (20) 'Joseph's dream' (Genesis 37:5–9). Joseph is asleep in a large bed covered with a green and pink blanket. Above him are twelve sheaves bowing to a large sheaf in the middle. On top is a human-faced, blazing red sun and a blue crescent moon. The stars are not represented.

fol. 5r, c (21) Joseph relating his dreams to his father and brothers. On a background of a large green building, the small figure of Joseph on the left tells his dreams to Jacob, who is seated in the middle. Inscribed 'And his father rebuked him' (Genesis 37:10). On the right are the figures of seven men, inscribed 'Joseph's brothers'.

fol. 5r, d, right (22) Joseph meets an angel on the way to his brothers (based on *Genesis Rabbah* 84:14). A winged angel shows the way to Joseph, who is carrying his dusky gold and vermilion garment on a stick over his shoulder. Inscribed 'And a certain man found him' (Genesis 37:15).

fol. 5r, d, left (23) '[His brethren] pasture the flock' (based on Genesis 37:12, 18). Six brothers are seated, some of them pointing towards Joseph, who is approaching. Behind them is a dog, and in front of them are three ewes and a ram. The scene is separated from scene 22 by a tree.

fol. 6v, a, right (24) The brothers' second council (Genesis 37:26–27). Five people are conversing behind a hilltop, one of them pointing at scene 25.

fol. 6v, a, left (25) Joseph is being pulled up from a round well by two of his brothers (Genesis 37:28). Wrongly inscribed 'And they cast him into a pit' (Genesis 37:24). The scene is separated from scene 24 by a tree.

fol. 6v, a, below left (26) Smearing Joseph's coat with blood. One brother, kneeling, holds a bleeding kid over Joseph's dusky gold garment, which is held by another brother. On the right two ewes and a ram graze. Inscribed on the right 'And they killed a kid of goats' (Genesis 37:31).

The three scenes in this compartment (24–26) are misplaced: the smearing of Joseph's coat should come after Joseph is sold to thc Ishmaelites (27).

fol. 6v, b (27) 'A company of Ishmaelites came...and they sold Joseph' (Genesis 37:25, 28). On the right is Joseph being passed over by one of his brothers to a Saracen dressed in white, while another Saracen puts handfuls of coins into the outer garment of another brother. To the left are two loaded mules.

fol. 6v, c (28) 'And they brought the coat of many colours to their father... and he rent his clothes' (based on Genesis 37:32, 24). To the left is Jacob, seated on a wide chair under a green canopy, tearing his clothes; his face is averted from Joseph's bloody dusky gold coat, which is held by one of the four brothers on the right. To the left of Jacob stands a mourning woman.

fol. 6v, d, top right (29) Joseph and Potiphar's wife. In a low-beamed room a crowned woman wearing underclothes is sitting up in bed and seizing the fleeing Joseph by his cloak. Inscribed, below to the right, 'And she caught him by his garment' (Genesis 39:12).

fol. 6v, d, top left (30) Potiphar and two of his friends hurry home through the open gate (not recorded in the Bible). No inscription.

fol. 6v, d, below (31) 'The dream of the butler and the baker' (Genesis 40:9–19). To the right is the butler, seated under a bent tree bearing clusters of grapes, squeezing one of the clusters into a cup. In the middle is the baker, a raven pecking at the loaves in a basket on his head. Joseph, bearded, is sitting on the left pointing at them with both hands. Inscribed 'Joseph interprets'.

וישחטו שעיר עזים
וישליכו אותו
ארחת ישמעאלים באה
וימכרו את יוסף
ויביאו את כתנת הפסים אל אביהם
קרע את בגדיו
ותתפשהו בבגדו
חלום המשקה והאופה
יוסף פותר

Fig. 21

7
חלום פרעה
חרטמי פרעה
ויגלח ויחלף שמלותיו
יוסף מדבר קשות לאחיו
ויאסר אותו לעיניהם

Fig. 22

fol. 7r, a (32) 'Pharaoh's dreams' of the cows and the ears of corn (Genesis 41:2–7). A crowned and bearded Pharaoh is asleep in a large bed. Above him are seven fat and seven lean red and brown cows and ears of corn.

fol. 7r, b (33) Joseph interpreting Pharaoh's dream in front of his counsellors. To the left, under a green canopy, the crowned and bearded Pharaoh is sitting on the same bench as a bearded Joseph and conversing with him. Inscribed 'And he shaved himself and changed his raiment' (Genesis 41:14). To the right stand three counsellors, also conversing, inscribed 'Pharaoh's magicians'.

fol. 7r, c (34) 'Joseph speaks roughly to his brothers' (based on Genesis 42:7) and orders the arrest of Simeon (Genesis 42:24). To the right is Joseph, seated before a curtain and pointing at four brothers, who are standing on the left. One of the brothers' hands are raised in astonishment. At their feet are a sack and Simeon, kneeling barefoot, his hands being bound by a servant. Inscribed 'And he bound him before their eyes' (Genesis 42:24).

fol. 7r, d (34) Joseph makes himself known to his brethren. To the right is Joseph, seated before a curtain and kissing a tiny Benjamin who stands on Joseph's knees. Inscribed 'And he fell upon his brother Benjamin's neck' (Genesis 45:14). Five brothers are approaching from the left.

fol. 8v, a (36) Jacob meets Pharaoh. Pharaoh, Jacob and Joseph are seated in front of a green baldachin to the left. To the right, behind a mountain, are three of 'Joseph's brothers'. In the bottom right-hand corner is a river with fishes. Inscribed 'And Joseph blessed Pharaoh' (Genesis 47:7, 10).

fol. 8v, b (37) 'He crossed his hands' to bless Ephraim and Manasseh (Genesis 48:1, 14). 'Jacob is sick', sitting up in bed on the left, propped up by a dusky gold decorated cushion. Behind him a curtain is hanging from the top of the panel. Jacob's hands are crossed over the kneeling children, behind whom are Joseph and three other men.

fol. 8v, c (38) Mourning over Jacob's bier. Jacob's coffin, covered by a purple cloth, stands under a tree. To the right kneel six mourners, one bearded, dressed in brown and blue monk's habits with capuchin hoods. To the left sit the other mourners: a crowned king and four bare-headed men. Inscribed 'And they came to the threshing floor of Atad' (Genesis 50:10).

fol. 8v, d, left (39) 'And Pharaoh said unto the midwives' that they should kill the male babies of the Hebrews (based on Exodus 1:15). Pharaoh, sitting on his throne, gives orders to two standing midwives. A counsellor is seated at his feet.

fol. 8v, d, right (40) 'Every son that is born ye shall cast into the river' (Exodus 1:22). In the bottom right-hand corner a bearded man is throwing a naked child into the river, where another child is drowning.

Scenes 39–40 should be read from left to right, as described above.

Fig. 23

ותתצב אחותו
ונערותיה הולכות
בתיה מביאה משה לפני פרעה
איש מצרי מכה איש עברי
ויך את המצרי ויטמנהו בחול

Fig. 24

fol. 9r, a (41) The finding of Moses. Miriam is seated on top of a hillock to the right. Inscribed 'And his sister stood' (Exodus 2:4). In the lower part of the panel, in the water, three naked maidens approach from the left. Inscribed 'And her maidens walked' (Exodus 2:5). The maiden in front is opening the lid of a box in which the infant Moses lies in swaddling clothes.

fol. 9r, b (42) 'Bitiah brings Moses before Pharaoh' (Pharaoh's daughter's name is not recorded in the Bible; based on *Leviticus Rabbah* 1:3). On the right is Pharaoh's daughter escorted by two maidens and carrying the swaddled infant Moses to show to the king enthroned on the left, listening to the advice of three counsellors (alluding to *Exodus Rabbah* 1:26).

fol. 9r, c, right (43) 'An Egyptian smites a Hebrew' (Exodus 2:11), using a club. Both are standing.

fol. 9r, c, left (44) 'He slew the Egyptian and hid him in the sand' (Exodus 2:12). The beardless Moses is holding an axe dripping with blood over a dead Egyptian, who is lying on the ground. The scene is separated from scene 43 by a tree.

fol. 9r, d (45) Moses saves the daughters of the priest of Midian. A beardless Moses, standing in the middle, is flanked by two trees. Behind him to his left are three women, one of them carrying a distaff. Moses prevents two male shepherds from interfering with the sheep drinking water from a spring below. Inscribed 'But Moses stood up and helped them' (Exodus 2:17).

fol. 10v, a, top right and left (46) A winged and nimbed angel appears above a burning bush on a mountain to the left (Exodus 3:2). Inscribed 'The angel of the bush'. On the right stands Moses, with his shoes on, lifting a covered hand to hide his face. Inscribed 'And Moses hid his face' (Exodus 3:6).

fol. 10v, a, centre (47) 'Put off thy shoes' (Exodus 3:5). In the middle of the panel Moses is sitting taking off his shoes. Below him are many sheep, a dog and a goat.

The sequence of this section may be taken from left to right: the angel on the extreme left (Exodus 3:2), Moses taking off his shoes (Exodus 3:5), and Moses hiding his face on the right (Exodus 3:6).

fol. 10v, b, right (48) Moses takes his family back to Egypt. Zipporah, approaching on horseback from the right, is carrying two babies in her arm; a dog walks alongside the horse. Inscribed 'And set them upon an ass' (Exodus 4:20).

fol. 10v, b, left (49) 'And Aaron met him' (based on Exodus 4:27). A bearded Aaron, appearing from the left, embraces a beardless Moses, who is carrying a lance and pointing to his wife on the horse.

fol. 10v, c (50) Moses and Aaron perform miracles before the Elders of Israel. On the right is a bearded Aaron holding a snake in his left hand; near him a beardless Moses points to the snake and expounds the miracle. Inscribed 'And he did the signs in the sight of the people' (Exodus 4:30). To the left are nine elders stretching out their hands, two of them kneeling. Inscribed 'Then they bowed their heads and worshipped' (Exodus 4:31). A blood-red spring separates the elders from Moses and Aaron.

fol. 10v, d (51) 'Moses and Aaron come before Pharaoh and his wise men' (Exodus 5:1–5). Aaron, with a long beard, and Moses, with a short beard and carrying a staff, appear before the enthroned Pharaoh, who is seated with legs crossed beneath a canopy holding a long sceptre with a fleur-de-lys at its end. Two counsellors are seated and another is standing in front of the king.

Fig. 25

Fig. 26

fol. 11r. a (52) The bondage of the Israelites (Exodus 5:6–13). To the right, at the top of a tower, is 'the taskmaster of the people', holding a stick. Below him are a barefoot old man carrying a bundle of straw and another barefoot man, 'the mixer of the clay', holding a stick. To the left are 'the maker of bricks', a woman carrying a baby to be put into the brick (based on *Exodus Rabbah* 5:22), and another woman.

fol. 11r, b (53) 'And they built for Pharaoh treasure cities' (Exodus 1:11). On the right is the taskmaster, holding a stick and giving instructions to two barefoot men on a scaffolding who are building a wall. Another barefoot man is raising a bucket by a pulley.

fol. 11r, c (54) 'But Aaron's rod swallowed up their rods' (Exodus 7:12). On the right is Aaron, holding a snake that is swallowing two other snakes held by two magicians. The magicians are seated at the feet of Pharaoh, enthroned, legs crossed, on the left. Another attendant stands to his left. Moses, who is standing in the middle, is arguing with them.

fol. 11r, d (55) The plague of blood. To the right are 'Moses and Aaron', the latter touching with his staff the red water of the river in which three dead fish are floating. On the left is Pharaoh, enthroned. Behind him, towards the centre, are two men digging for water with hoes and finding blood. Inscribed '[And all the Egyptians digged round about the river for water to drink]' (Exodus 7:24).

fol. 12v, a (56) The plague of frogs. On the right 'Moses' (not Aaron, as in the Bible), with a short beard, touches the water with his staff. A row of green frogs leap out of the water into vessels in a cabinet, into windows – in one of which there is a figure – and on to Pharaoh, who is seated on his throne on the left before a curtain. Inscribed 'And the frogs came up' (Exodus 8:2; A.V. 8:6).

fol. 12v, b (57) The plague of lice. 'Aaron', touching the ground with his staff, and 'Moses', on the right, appear before the enthroned Pharaoh and two of his wise men, who are all covered with lice. To the right are a donkey scratching its muzzle and two bulls. To the left, at windows above Pharaoh and the magicians, are three women scratching themselves, two of them with double ivory combs. Inscribed 'And it became lice in man and in beast' (Exodus 8:13; A.V. 8:17).

fol. 12v, c (58) 'A grievous *'arov'* (Exodus 8:20; A.V. 8:24), i.e. beasts (based on *Exodus Rabbah* 11:4; *Midrash Tanḥuma, Parashat Bo*). 'Moses', holding a staff, stands on the right before Pharaoh, who is standing in front of a baldachin accompanied by an attendant. A squirrel, a dog, a lion, a wolf and a griffon are stepping over each other and attacking the astonished Pharaoh.

fol. 12v, d (59) 'A very grievous murrain' (Exodus 9:3). In the middle, from the top of a crenellated tower, one youth is lowering a dead sheep and another a dead goat. On the ground surrounding the tower are dead horses and cattle. To the right a man is wiping away a tear. To the left is another man, inscribed 'Rending his garments'.

Fig. 27

Fig. 28

fol. 13r, a (60) The plague of boils. To the right 'Moses throws the ashes of the furnace' (based on Exodus 9:10) out of a bowl. The ashes are depicted as red dots. Behind Moses is Aaron, holding a staff. To the left is 'a physician who comes before Pharaoh', who is enthroned, barefoot and covered with spots. Below are two seated counsellors, a shepherd, sheep and a donkey, all of them covered with spots.

fol. 13r, b, left (61) The plague of 'hail and flaming fire' (Exodus 9:24). From a segment of blue sky above fall white and red dots, breaking the branches of a tree under which are a hooded shepherd, sheep and a goat. To the left is Pharaoh on his throne.

fol. 13r, b, right (62) Moses begs God to stop the plague of hail. Moses, standing, 'spreads abroad his hands unto the Lord' (Exodus 9:33).

Scenes 61–62 should be read from left to right, as described above.

fol. 13r, c (63) The plague of 'locusts' (Exodus 10:13–15). To the right are 'Moses and Aaron', the former touching the ground with his staff, from which locusts are creeping up two trees.

fol. 13r, d, top (64) The plague of 'thick darkness' (Exodus 10:22). On the left, on a dark brown background, are the king and three seated men. To the right are a boy and two men feeling their way in the darkness. A bird is sitting on a perch.

fol. 13r, d, below (65) 'And they spoiled the Egyptians' (Exodus 12:36). Four Israelites, three of them barefoot, are taking three gold chalices from an open cupboard. One is carrying a chest on his back, supporting it with raised hands.

The relationship between the last two scenes is based on *Exodus Rabbah* 14:3 and 1:12.

fol. 14v, a, top (66) 'The plague of the firstborn' (Exodus 12:29–30). On the right, in a domed room, is a winged angel swinging his sword and smiting a man in bed. A woman stands mourning at the side. To the left sits the crowned queen, mourning her son, who lies in a nurse's lap.

fol. 14v, a, below (67) The funeral of the firstborn (not recorded in the Bible) or, The Israelites taking Joseph's bier out of Egypt (Exodus 13:19). Six men are carrying a covered coffin. In front are three mourners wearing brown monk's habits.

fol. 14v, b (68) Pharaoh commands the Israelites to leave Egypt. To the right, on top of a battlemented wall, is the king, with two counsellors, pointing outwards with his hand. Inscribed 'Rise up and get you forth' (Exodus 12:31). Walking towards the left are the Israelites, their right hands raised. Some of them hold lumps of dough, and a woman is carrying a baby. Moses follows behind holding his staff. Inscribed 'And the Children of Israel went out with a high hand' (Exodus 14:8).

fol. 14v, c (69) The pursuit by the Egyptians. An army of mounted knights, headed by the crowned king, is riding towards the left, all of them carrying lances. The king's banner, shield and the housing of his horse are *azure* with a lion *rampant or* (Leon). Other escutcheons are: *gules*, a ring and a blazing sun *or* and *azure*; a wing *or* and *gules*; and a lion *rampant or*. Inscribed 'And Pharaoh drew nigh' (Exodus 14:10).

fol. 14v, d (70) The passage of the Red Sea. The Israelites are on the left, surrounded by water. One of them carries a child on his shoulder and a woman carries a baby in her arms. Moses follows behind them, holding a staff and turning round to look at the drowning king, horses and soldiers, who are surrounded by fish. Inscribed 'And the Lord overthrew the Egyptians in the midst of the sea' (Exodus 14:27).

Fig. 29

Fig. 30

fol. 15r, a (71) 'And Miriam the prophetess, the sister of Aaron, took the timbrel in her hand' (Exodus 15.20). Five girls are playing musical instruments: a lute, a square and a round timbrel, cymbals and sticks. Two girls are dancing.

2. *Ritual Scenes*

fol. 15r, b (72) 'The master of the house orders *mazoth* and *ḥaroṣet* (sweetmeat) to be given to the children'. On the left the master of the house is seated under a canopy and pointing with his hand. On a bridge on the right is a group of five children and a woman carrying a baby, some holding round *mazoth*. Two other children serve them, one carrying a basket over his shoulder, the other holding plates of *ḥaroṣet*, which is being served from a pot by a man sitting on the left, below the master of the house.

fol. 15r, c, right (73) 'He searcheth out the leaven by the light of a candle'. A bearded man holding a lighted yellow candle is reaching into a niche with a stick to clear out the leaven into a bowl being held by a youth.

fol. 15r, c, left (74) '[She sweeps the house and cleans it]'. A woman is cleaning the coffered ceiling with a long-handled brush. In the middle is a girl sweeping the floor with a small brush.

Scenes 73–74 are depicted inside one room, with many niches and a coffered ceiling.

fol. 15r, d, right (75) 'Making preparations for Passover'. In a house with a coffered ceiling a man is slaughtering a sheep on the ground, while another skins a ram that is hanging, together with a skinned sheep, from a rod below the ceiling.

fol. 15r, d, left (76) Cleansing dishes. Beneach a baldachin a man is putting dishes into a large black cauldron over the fire.

THE ARTISTS OF THE BIBLICAL MINIATURES

Two artists can be distinguished in the painting of the full-page miniatures. Yet, in spite of individual differences, it is quite obvious that both belonged to the same north-eastern Spanish workshop, probably in Barcelona, and that both had common models from which to copy: their idiosyncrasies in manner and expression may be attributed to personal differences in training and talent. Each of the artists was given one quire to illustrate, so that the first illuminated the Genesis episodes and five panels of Exodus (fols. 2v–9), while the other illustrated the rest of Exodus and the three ritual scenes (fols. 10v–15).

This second artist is by far the better of the two. His drawings of the human figure, natural objects and architecture are firm and sure. He is fully acquainted with the northern French technique of rendering naked parts of the body, drapery, and stereotyped oval faces with hardly any change in expression. All these are common features in most French schools of illumination, as well as in the north-eastern Spanish school, which was dependent on the northern French school, at the end of the thirteenth and the beginning of the fourteenth centuries. However, the exaggerated hand gestures with large palms and fingers, the large heads in proportion to the small bodies, and the high wide foreheads and narrowing chins stand out as more personal features in the style of the second artist.

Both use the same technique in rendering draperies and faces, but the first artist is less successful. He does not seem to be so sure of his outlines, his drapery is stiffer, and the human form lacks the elegance of the Parisian style which he is attempting to imitate. The naked parts of the body are clumsily drawn, with little interest in their shape. Hands, fingers, legs and heads are twisted and out of proportion, although the exaggerated gestures are similar to those used by the second artist. Hair styles are not puffed out and are drawn with thicker lines, sometimes giving them an untidy look. The heads incline forward, with large eyes and pupils slanting sideways, stressing the intensity of their gaze. The somewhat flattened noses are particularly evident in profiles. Faces as drawn by the first artist are more expressive, though the expression does not always suit the occasion. In the stabbing scene near the Tower of Babel (fol. 3), for instance, attackers and victims both have the same calm air. More convincing is the expression of mourning on the woman's face in the miniature of Jacob being shown Joseph's bloody garment (fol. 6v). The first artist's trees are clusters of leaves on straight trunks. His cleft, stepped ground, dotted with tufts of grass, betrays the Byzantine artistic origins of its prototype.

Such a personal, inferior style makes it difficult to identify the first artist with any particular school. The many similarities between the two artists make it clear, however, that both belong to the same environment and the same workshop. This is a Spanish atelier influenced by two definite styles: northern French and Italian.

Good examples for comparing both artists of the Haggadah are folios 3, by the first artist (fig. 18), and 11, by the second (fig. 26). In composition all the picture panels by the second artist (fol. 11) are well balanced, leaving ample space between the figures so as to suggest depth. Smaller figures are painted on top of buildings and in the background, such as the diggers in the bottom left panel. On folio 3, by the first artist, three panels are too compressed and full of detail, whereas the top right panel leaves too large a space as background, unbalancing the composition. The architectural details of the second artist (fol. 11) suggest a more accurate illusion of perspective than the first's. The second artist uses a single viewpoint for edifices, and observes the composition in the picture panel from one angle only, usually from above (though sometimes from below, as in the ritual panels on folio 15). To obscure inaccuracies, he covers the lower parts of buildings with uneven ground or figures. The first artist uses several viewpoints in the same panel, both for buildings and in composition. The house in which Sarah stands (fol. 3, lower left) is seen from the right, from the left, and from above; the Tower of Babel is seen from below and above; Nimrod's throne is actually a rectangular frame, compared with the baldachins beneath which the second artist's Pharaoh is seated on folio 11.

The swaying human body and its gestures are more naturalistically rendered by the second artist (fol. 11). His figures are well proportioned compared with the small, stocky creatures of the first artist (fol. 3). Limbs can be identified, and movements are much clearer. The gesture of the man working the pulley at the upper left of folio 11 should be compared with that of the man mixing mortar with a hoe near the Tower of Babel (fol. 3, upper left). The second artist's palm gestures are pronounced and exaggerated, whereas the first artist exaggerates the facial expressions. If we compare the seated kings in both miniatures, we see that the second artist's drapery seems much softer, more delicate and elegant, suggesting a body under it, in contrast to the thick heavy folds of the first artist.

The northern French elements of the Golden Haggadah's miniatures are to be found in the structure, composition and figure style. Series of full-page miniatures, divided into framed panels with diapered and studded tooled gold backgrounds, are typical of the French biblical pictures sometimes found in Latin psalters between the calendar and the psalter proper, or in *La Somme le Roi* manuscripts of the thirteenth and fourteenth centuries.[29] The division of miniatures into four panels with the composition filling the entire space can be compared to the Pierpont Morgan Picture Bible of *c.* 1250,[30] or to the manuscript of *La Somme le Roi* attributed to Master Honoré of *c.* 1300.[31]

The Haggadah artists did not work in the pronounced style of Honoré, though some general affinities with the master and his followers can be mentioned: puffed-out wavy hair, expressive oval faces, heavy folded drapery, inclination of the body, gestures, and colours.

Comparison of the lower left panel on folio 10v (fig. 25), by the second artist, with the miniature on the first page of a manuscript of Gratian's *Decretals* (Bibliothèque Municipale, Tours, MS. 558, fol. 1,

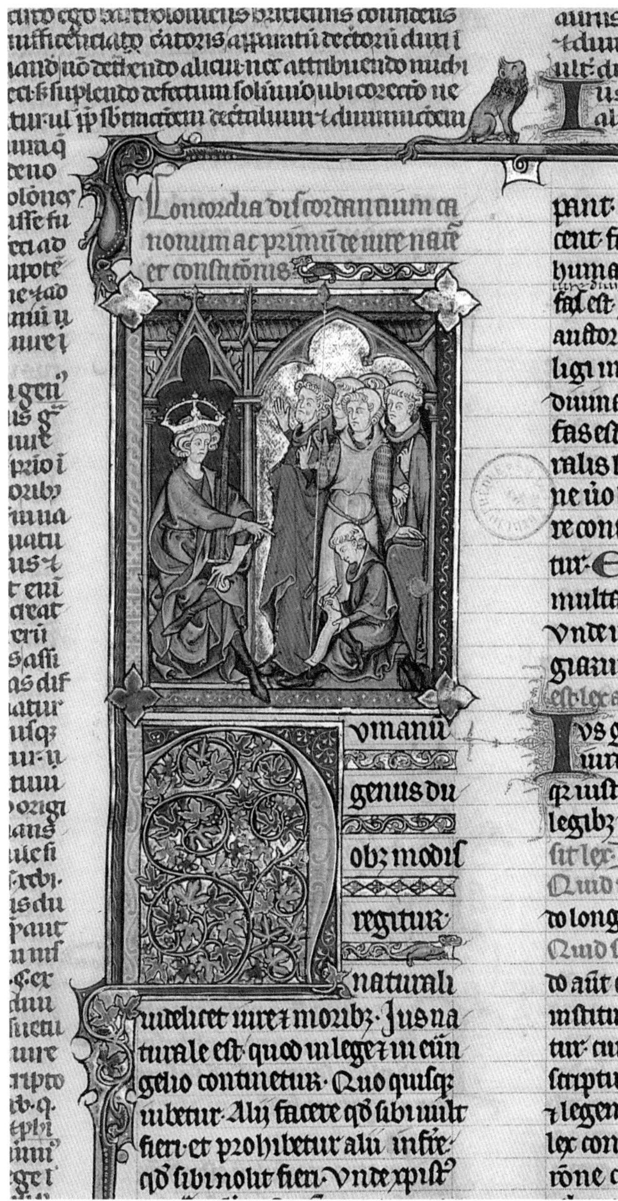

Fig. 31. A judge. Opening miniature of Gratian's *Decretals* by the illuminator Maître Honoré. Tours, Bibliothèque Municipale, MS. 558, fol. 1. (Detail).

fig. 31), the only work which mentions the illuminator Honoré by name, may prove profitable. The similar composition in both miniatures may be ascribed to the prevailing northern French style of the late thirteenth century. The fact that the panel in the Haggadah has no architectural framework makes it somewhat more advanced than the *Decretals*. Another manuscript attributed to Master Honoré, the Breviary of Philippe le Bel (Bibliothèque Nationale, Paris, MS. lat. 1023), also has no architectural frames to the panels.[32] Resemblances in figure style between the Haggadah and the *Decretals* are seen in the dramatic gestures, the puffed-out hair, the facial features, the way the drapery falls, and the dark outlines, although Honoré uses heavier shading and highlights. The architectural details are dissimilar, for Honoré renders a flat, decorative, French edifice, while the Haggadah artist renders an Italianate baldachin drawn in perspective.

The few Italianising elements in the style of the Haggadah miniatures could have reached both our Spanish artists either indirectly, through Italian influence on French illumination in the fourteenth century, or directly, through the use of a byzantinised Italian archetype. These Italian elements are, for instance, the softer drapery, the double-tendril linear decorations on exteriors and interiors of buildings, and the cleft ground dotted with tufts of grass.[33] This last element is more apparent on the first artist's pages, but also in folios 10v, 11 and 13 by the second artist. The step-like moulded ground is not merely a technical method of depicting rock formation: the first artist uses it as a means of creating space and depth in his miniatures. Good examples are in Noah's Vineyard on folio 3 and Casting Joseph into the Pit on folio 6v. In both cases this technique is also used to separate two scenes in one panel. The first artist did not succeed in creating the impression of depth in all his miniatures. Most of them show lack of understanding of this spatial technique (e.g. folios 4v, 5, 8v). It has to be assumed that the first artist aimed at great accuracy in copying his archetype, which contained this formula, but that he was not always successful. Such use of rock formations as a way of indicating space was known to most Italian artists who painted in the Greek manner.[34] The second artist also used the 'cleft ground' technique, not to imply depth, but rather as a decorative device to enliven the otherwise flat background. The Calling of Moses on folio 10v is a good example, following the French thirteenth-century manner, with foreground figures overlapping layers of background.

The Italian prototype which included this Byzantine

Fig. 32. A panel from Duccio di Buoninsegna, *Maestà*, 1308, showing an interior with a coffered ceiling. Siena, Museo dell'Opera del Duomo.

formula must have been an advanced one which used not only this form to create spatial illusion, but also the 'box-like' architectural background to indicate depth. These elements were apparent mainly in Bolognese and Neapolitan illumination of the period.[35] Most such backgrounds are low, elongated buildings with two sides visible, with small upper stories and round pinnacles on top of slanting roofs with their tiles overlapping like scales (on fols. 3–5, 9, 11, 12v and 15). This kind of architectural background, reminiscent of Italian painting of the thirteenth and fourteenth centuries,[36] is very different from the flat-façaded, perspectiveless, thirteenth-century French architectural framework. The best examples in our manuscript are all on folio 15, in the three ritual pictures. They are a throne with baldachin, and low, straight-beamed interiors with coffered ceilings. In using this technique the second artist manages to create a fairly good spatial illusion. Straight-beamed, coffered ceilings as a means of indicating space were already used by late thirteenth-century Italian artists such as Cavallini in his mosaics in Rome and by the so-called Isaac Master in Assisi,[37] and were developed further by Duccio (fig. 32), Giotto and Simone Martini. Though acquainted with the coffered ceiling device, which appears only in his baldachins (e.g. fols. 3, 7, 8v), the first artist did not use it to indicate space.

The Italian and French stylistic elements incorporated in the Golden Haggadah prove that at least two different models were used by the artists. The meeting of Italian Gothic style with French High Gothic elements could have taken place anywhere in western Europe at the beginning of the fourteenth century, from southern Italy to England, including Paris. In the case of the Golden Haggadah, Catalonia, and in particular Barcelona, should be taken into consideration. The famous *Vidal Major* of around 1280, now in the J. Paul Getty Museum in Malibu,[38] is too early to contain the same Italian elements as the Golden Haggadah.

The soft drapery, the 'cleft ground' and the 'coffered ceiling' devices first appear in Catalonia in the second quarter of the fourteenth century, in manuscripts such as the *Constitutions* of James II of Majorca of 1334, now in Brussels,[39] and the Catalan additions to the third copy of the Utrecht Psalter in Paris.[40] At the same time, the influence of a dominant Italian figure style was felt in Catalonia through the painting of Ferrer Bassa and the school of illumination of the Master of the *Privilegios* in Barcelona and Palma.[41] However, the completely Italianate figure style of these manuscripts is too late to be compared with the French figure style of the Golden Haggadah.

This combination of a distinct French style with sporadic Italianate elements is, indeed, known from the transitional period of illuminated manuscripts from north-eastern Spain and the south of France in the early fourteenth century. The nearest in style is a manuscript of Catalan Laws in Paris.[42] This manuscript is a collection of ten different texts written and illuminated by different hands at different dates. The parts which chiefly relate to our Haggadah are items 7 and 9 in the table of contents: the *Usatici Barcinonenses* on folios 67–117, and the *Consuetudines Cataloniae editae per Petrum Alberti* on folios 123–238v, all issued by James II of Aragon. These two treatises are illustrated and have ten panels, mainly depicting kings in council. The illustrations are in the Catalan style, with pronounced French influence, while their Catalan origin is guaranteed by the nature of the text. They were painted by two artists, probably from the Catalan court school, at the beginning of the fourteenth century. Since the latest act copied in the original hand of the manuscript is dated 1321, it can be assumed that the miniatures were executed at about the same time and in any case not later than 1337, the date of the subsequent first entry in the later hand. Of the two artists in lat. 4670A, the first is closer in style to the second artist of the Golden Haggadah (fol. 67, fig. 33). The puffed-out hair, the oval faces, the sunken cheeks drawn with a "V" sign, the elegant sway of the body, the folds of the drapery, the keen interest in naked parts of the body, the exaggerated finger and hand gestures and the rendering of profiles are similar in both artists. Some other details are common to them both, for instance the cleft ground, the baldachin-like throne, smaller upper stories of buildings, the double-arched windows, the lanceolate battlements, the Italianate double-tendril decorations on walls, the row of arched recesses under thrones, the

Fig. 33. A king and queen in council, probably James II of Aragon issuing laws in Barcelona. *Usatici Barcionenses*, 1321. Paris, Bibliothèque Nationale, lat. 4670A, fol. 67. (Detail).

canopied throne hung with draperies which are tucked under tasselled cushions beneath the ruler's feet, crowns, armour, hats and kerchiefs. Even the diapered background and the delicate rinceaux in the frames are similarly rendered and have the same pattern in the *Usatici* as in the Golden Haggadah. Besides the style and the iconographical details, a further most striking similarity between the two manuscripts is the composition of the miniatures and the grouping of figures, especially noticeable in courtly scenes.[43]

All these similarities tend to point to Barcelona as the place of execution of the Golden Haggadah, which was probably illuminated in a workshop connected with the royal court which also illuminated the *Usatici* of James II; and to a date around 1320 but not later than 1335. This date accords with the general development of illuminated manuscripts in France and in Spain. This was a transitional period, when Italian spatial concepts began to influence manuscript illumination in the west. Before 1320 these spatial concepts were not well established, and after 1335 the Italian figure style became dominant both in France and in Catalonia.[44]

THE MODELS FOR THE BIBLICAL MINIATURES

The Lay-out of Illuminated Psalters

The full-page biblical miniatures attached to the text of the Spanish Haggadoth resemble to a great extent the similar large range of full-page biblical miniatures attached to Latin psalter manuscripts of the Gothic period. Illuminated psalters of this type developed in England and France during the twelfth and thirteenth centuries and may have been based on earlier Byzantine aristocratic psalters. These psalters from the post-iconoclastic period traditionally had full-page miniatures depicting various episodes from the life of David, the main composer and protagonist of the psalms; however, episodes from the lives of Moses or other biblical figures were sometimes included when they were related to various psalms and additional prayers. These miniatures were inserted in the appropriate places at the main divisions of the Book of Psalms.

The creators of the English and French psalters gathered the miniatures into one continuous sequence preceding the text of the psalter, after the annual calendar. They arranged the episodes in chronological order and added episodes from the life of Christ, implying that Moses and David were prototypes of Christ. Following the same theological scheme, they added episodes from the lives of Joseph and the Patriarchs. Episodes from the life of Adam and Eve were also inserted, probably in order to stress the role of Christ as Redeemer from original sin.

Gradually a chronological sequence of full-page biblical illustrations developed as an essential part of the Gothic illuminated psalter. These illustrations consisted of a variety of pictures, sometimes starting with the creation of the world, continuing with episodes from the Old and New Testaments, and ending with the Last Judgement. The selection of episodes in these full-page miniatures was left to the discretion of the artist or the patron, and its expansion probably depended on the financial position of the latter. Having a short text with contents appropriate for private devotion, the illuminated psalter became a very popular book all over western Europe during the thirteenth and fourteenth centuries. Influenced mainly by the French royal school in Paris, such sumptuous psalters were produced in many countries, such as Spain, Germany and the Netherlands, besides France and England, their size ranging from giant volumes to minute pocket books, depending on their use. Besides forming a decorative addition to the psalter, these biblical illustrations may have served as educational material for the young in the royal, courtly or affluent urban families which owned them.

The Lay-out of Sephardi Illuminated Haggadoth

The full-page biblical miniatures in the Haggadoth seem to have been directly influenced by the western illuminated psalter manuscripts. They are structured in the same way, with a continuous collection of full-page biblical miniatures preceding the text of the Haggadah, and possibly serving a similar educational purpose. These Haggadoth were produced for affluent Jewish families connected with Christian royal and aristocratic families which owned similar sumptuous manuscripts. In imitating the cultural habits of these Christian nobles, the Jews chose to illustrate the Haggadah rather than the psalter with biblical pictures, probably because the Haggadah was by then a private book used at home, relating the essential history of the creation of Israel as a nation. The main subjects chosen to illustrate the Haggadah were therefore the Bondage of the Israelites in Egypt and their Exodus. The scope of the series of miniatures was sometimes broadened, as in the late fourteenth-century Sarajevo Haggadah,[45] to begin with the creation of the world and end with Moses blessing Israel before his death.

Such Haggadoth may have been produced in France

during the thirteenth century, although none has survived. The public burning of the Talmud and other Hebrew books in Paris in 1240 and the first expulsion of the Jews from the French kingdom in 1306 may have been partly responsible for their loss. By the end of the thirteenth century and the beginning of the fourteenth, sumptuous illuminated Haggadoth of this type had spread to Provence in the south of France and to north-eastern Spain. Three of the eleven Haggadoth with full-page biblical miniatures may have been produced in the thirteenth century in Spain or Provence,[46] namely that in Parma,[47] that in the Biblioteca Casanatense in Rome,[48] and the Hispano-Moresque Haggadah in the British Library.[49] All three reveal an archaic style, which may point to the use of an earlier model dating from the beginning of the thirteenth century.

Christian Iconography in the Haggadoth

Some of the episodes depicted in the Haggadoth seem to have been taken directly from Christian illuminated psalters. One example is by the first artist of the Golden Haggadah, depicting Moses and the Burning Bush (fol. 10v, top right, fig. 25), where Moses is seen twice: once approaching, and again sitting taking off his shoes. A very similar representation can be seen in the Morgan Picture Bible,[50] which is probably a collection of full-page miniatures intended to be attached to a psalter. Obviously, instead of Christ appearing within the flames of the burning bush as in the Morgan Picture Bible (fol. 7v, fig. 34), the Haggadah miniature has an angel, as stated in the Bible and in accordance with the Jewish belief. Similarly, the Golden Haggadah's Creation of Eve, showing her emerging from Adam's side while he sleeps, and the Temptation of Adam by Eve where they

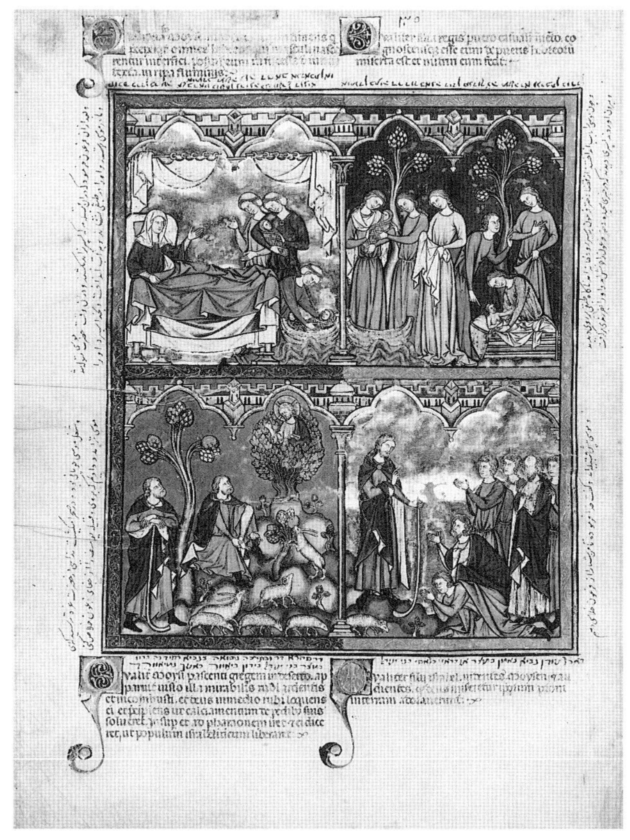

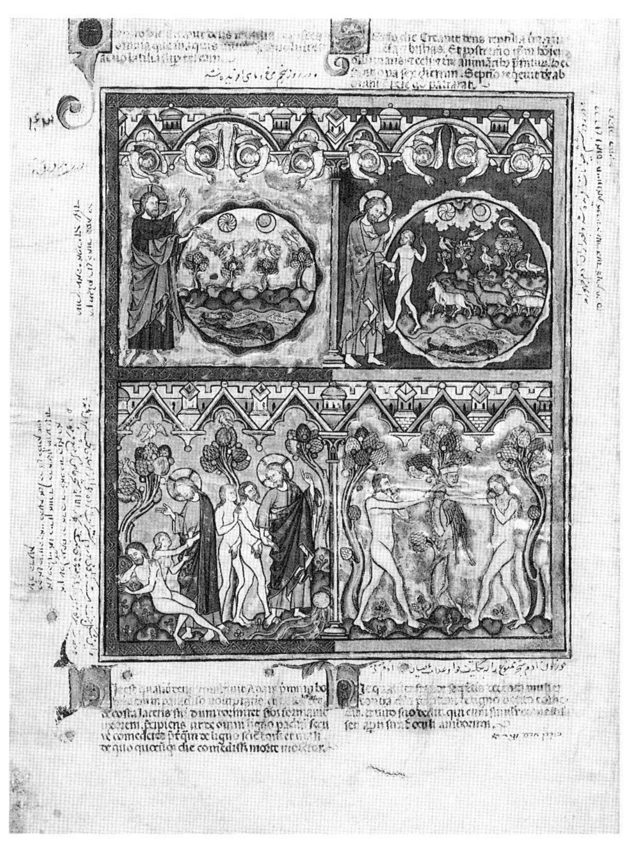

Fig. 34. (*Right, above*) The story of Moses, including Moses before the Burning Bush. Morgan Picture Bible, Paris, end of thirteenth century. New York, Pierpont Morgan Library, ms. 638, fol. 7v.

Fig. 35. (*Right, below*) The last days of Creation, including the creation of Eve from Adam's side and the Temptation of Adam and Eve by the serpent. Morgan Picture Bible, Paris, end of thirteenth century. New York, Pierpont Morgan Library, ms. 638, fol. 1v.

both flank a tree (fol. 2v, top left, fig. 17) show that the artist must have been acquainted with the traditional Christian iconography, which also appears in the Morgan Picture Bible (fol. 1v, fig. 35)[51].

A further example of direct Christian influence on the iconography of the Golden Haggadah is in the picture of Moses meeting his brother Aaron on his way back to Egypt. Moses is shown as a youth walking in front of the horse ridden by his wife Zipporah with their two children in her arms; confronting them is the bearded Aaron (fol. 10v, top left, fig. 25). This rendering resembles the traditional iconography of the Flight into Egypt with Mary carrying Christ on a donkey led by Christ's step-brother, the youth James, and accompanied by the bearded Joseph.

Many other episodes in the Golden Haggadah and other Haggadoth seem to derive from the traditional repertoire of Christian biblical illustrations, the most telling being Moses and Aaron announcing the Ten Plagues to Pharaoh, who is seated as a king in his court.

Christian and Jewish Renderings of the same Subject

Some of the Ten Plagues depicted in the Haggadoth contain a different iconography from the common Christian biblical illustrations. For example, the Fourth Plague, called *'Arov*, is an ambiguous term even in the Hebrew Bible. The rabbis interpreted it as meaning a 'multitude (= many kinds, mélange) of wild beasts' (*Exodus Rabbah* 11:4), while the Greek Septuagint and the Latin Vulgate called it 'a multitude (= many kinds) of flies' (*omne genus muscarum* in Latin, Exodus 8:21). Thus in the Golden Haggadah (fol. 12v, bottom right, fig. 27) and in all other Haggadoth the artists depict lions, wolves or even squirrels and dragons attacking the Egyptians, whereas in the Christian illustrations such as the St Louis Psalter[52] flies are represented. However, in a twin Christian picture Bible from Pamplona both flies and beasts appear, implying that the artist knew both traditions and did not wish to choose between them. They appear in the two large full-page Pamplona Picture Bibles made for King Sancho el Fuerte of Navarre, who reigned from 1194–1234. In the Amiens version (fig. 36) the beasts are depicted after the plague of lice (*cinifes* in Latin);[53] whereas in the Harburg version flies appear inscribed *muscas* (Vulgate, Exodus 8:24) instead of lice, and no beasts are shown.[54] The Latin Pamplona Bibles contain several other Jewish midrashic interpretations in their miniatures.

Jewish Interpretations in Christian Illustrations

Another midrashic interpretation which appears in the Pamplona Bibles as well as in the Spanish Haggadoth consists of three naked women in the waters of the Nile 'finding Moses' (Golden Haggadah, fol. 9, top right,

Fig. 36. The plague of lice and the plague of *'Arov* (shown as beasts and wrongly inscribed as the plague of murrain). Pamplona Picture Bible of King Sancho el Fuerte of Navarre, 1194–1234. Amiens, Bibliothèque Municipale, lat. 108, fol. 43.

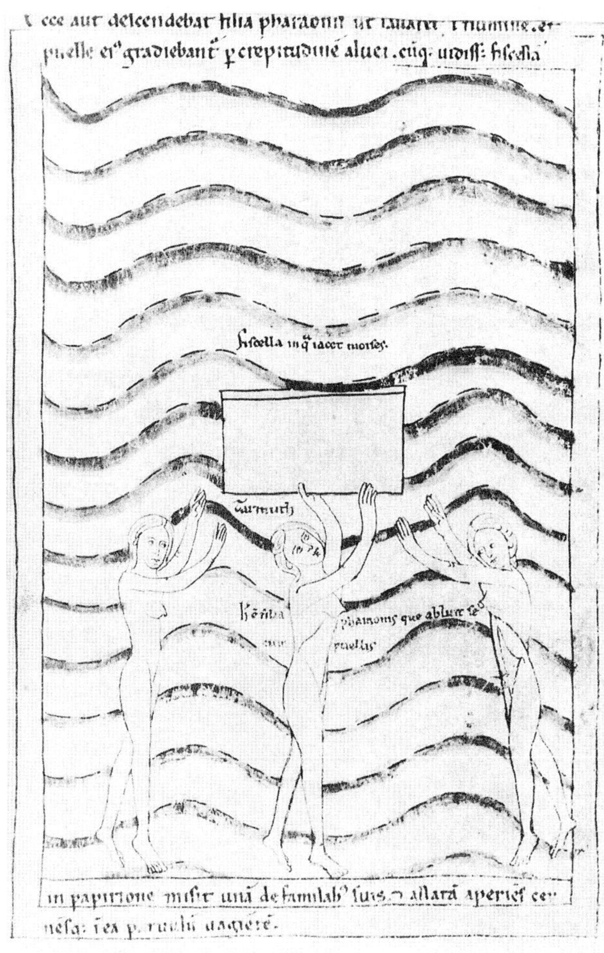

Fig. 37. Tarmuth, Pharaoh's daughter, and her two maidens find Moses in his ark while bathing in the Nile. Pamplona Picture Bible, Navarre, 1194–1234. Harburg, Prince Öttingen-Wallerstein Collection, ms. 1.2, fol. 49.

fig. 24). The rabbis gave two interpretations (*Midrash Exodus Rabbah* 1:27; Babylonian Talmud, *Sota* 12b) regarding Pharaoh's daughter, which depend on the term *amatah* (Exodus 2:5), one being 'her maid' and the other 'her arm', both of which are correct in Hebrew. The latter interpretation seems more logical, since according to the Bible it was 'she who went down to bathe', while 'her maidens were walking on the shore'. However, the Septuagint and the Vulgate translate *amatah* as 'one of her maidens' (*unam e famulis suis*), and in most medieval Christian illustrations Pharaoh's daughter appears on the shore and a maiden is in the water, as in the St Louis Psalter.[55]

The princess does appear, crowned, in the water in some English and French Christian illuminations, as well as in most Jewish ones, bathing for ritual purification after being cured of her boils, and touching Moses' ark.[56] Two of the Sephardi Haggadoth stress the interpretation that Pharaoh's daughter herself found Moses: one is the Kaufmann Haggadah of the late fourteenth century,[57] where the compartment is divided into two. To the right are the three naked women with the crowned princess in front, and to the left she is handing the baby Moses to his sister and mother to nurse. The second is the Sarajevo Haggadah (fol. 20), where the crowned, clothed princess is standing in the water touching the ark. The rabbis considered her to be a believer in the true God and therefore some of them called her *Bitiah*, the 'daughter of God'. She is so inscribed in the next compartment of the Golden Haggadah (fol. 9, top left, fig. 24), where she is presenting Moses to Pharaoh. Another of her midrashic names, *Tarmuth*,[58] is inscribed above her in the second Pamplona Bible, executed before the end of the twelfth century (fig. 37),[59] obvious evidence of the direct

Fig. 38. Pharaoh's daughter and her maidens find Moses in his ark while bathing. French *Bible Historiée*, Paris, early fourteenth century. New York, Public Library, Spencer Collection ms. 22, fol. 39v. (Detail).

influence of a Jewish midrashic source. The fourteenth-century French *Bible Historiée* based on the Pamplona Bibles[60] depicts the three women in the water in a way similar to the Golden Haggadah (fig. 38).

Since there are many such midrashic elements in the Pamplona Bibles, the main question is, how did these elements reach the individual artists who created these Bibles, when no such Jewish illuminated manuscripts are extant? Did one of these Jewish manuscripts exist at the end of the twelfth century? Or was such an illustration already incorporated in earlier Christian manuscripts? If so, when was this Jewish iconography introduced into Christian illustrations? Is it possible to ascertain when and where such Jewish iconography evolved? Or was there a twelfth-century Christian theologian capable of instructing the artists to include so many midrashic elements in their picture Bibles? The answers to these questions may help to trace the origins and models of the Golden Haggadah.

Fig. 39. Pharaoh's daughter finds Moses while bathing in the Nile and gives him to Miriam. who gives him to his mother Jochebed. Wall painting from the west wall of the Synagogue at Dura Europos on the Euphrates, 244 AD. (Detail.) Damascus, National Museum. (Courtesy Princeton University Press.)

Early Jewish Biblical Illustrations

Strange as it may seem, the oldest representation of Pharaoh's daughter standing naked in the waters of the Nile and holding the naked Moses is found in the third-century wall painting from the Dura Europos synagogue. Her three maidens, dressed as nymphs, are standing on the shore, as well as Miriam and Jochebed, Moses' sister and mother (fig. 39).[61] Dating from 244 AD, the Dura synagogue paintings constitute some of the earliest preserved representations of biblical art. Moreover, besides illustrations of purely biblical texts, the wall paintings contain many elements which depend on Jewish midrashic interpretations.

It is implausible that all these biblical and midrashic illustrations originated in Dura Europos, a provincial garrison city on the borders of the Roman and Parthian empires: the artists must have had an illustrated model derived from one of the main Jewish centres of the time, such as Antioch or Alexandria. Such a model may have been an illuminated Greek or Aramaic manuscript of paraphrases of the Bible, similar to Josephus' *History of the Jews* or the *Pseudo-Jonathan Targum*, both of which include midrashic elements in their account of the biblical stories. Oral midrashic expositions of the Bible by different rabbis are known from the early Hellenistic period in the fourth century BC. The written *midrash* was compiled at different periods from the second to the twelfth centuries.

A further midrashic depiction from the Dura Europos synagogue is the Crossing of the Red Sea by twelve paths, one for each tribe, to avoid quarrels over precedence. Now known only from the late *Midrash* of *Pirkei d'Rabbi Eli'ezer* (ch. 42), it must have been known in Late Antiquity either through oral tradition or a now lost manuscript (fig. 40).[62] This midrashic episode is depicted in some Hebrew illuminated manuscripts of the thirteenth and fourteenth centuries, and is hinted at in four of the full-page illuminations of Sephardi Haggadoth. The earliest of these is the Casanatense

Fig. 40. (*Above*) The Israelites crossing the Red Sea by twelve paths. Wall painting from the west wall of the Dura Europos Synagogue on the Euphrates, 244 AD. Damascus, National Museum. (Courtesy Princeton University Press.)

Haggadah (Cod. 2761, fol. 4) of the thirteenth century, where the paths are shown as semi-circles, similar to how they appear in some Sephardi Bibles of around 1300. In the Rylands Haggadah[63] and its Brother,[64] both from the third quarter of the fourteenth century, only three and two straight paths respectively are represented, hinting at the rest; in the Sarajevo Haggadah[65] the two paths are curved.

Another midrashic episode shows Pharaoh saved from drowning because of his last-minute repentance.[66]

Interestingly, the twelve paths also appear in the Pamplona Bible (fig. 41).[67]

Fig. 41. (*Right*) The Israelites crossing the Red Sea by twelve paths. Pamplona Picture Bible, Navarre, 1194–1234. Harburg, Prince Öttingen-Wallerstein Collection, ms. 1. 2, fol. 57v.

How to Bridge the Gap

The interest of the Jews in their *midrashim* as illustrative material for synagogues and manuscripts is obvious, since the Jewish theological interpretations and the legendary episodes included in them cry out to be illustrated. It should be noted, however, that Jewish biblical illustrations only appear in the third century and then again, following a long gap, in the thirteenth and fourteenth centuries, with no possible direct link between them. How is this gap to be bridged, when no single Hebrew illuminated manuscript survives from before the thirteenth century? It is true that some biblical illustrations, mainly in synagogues, survive from as late as the sixth century, for example the Sacrifice of Isaac in the mosaic floor of the Beit Alpha synagogue, but despite this the time gap is too wide. One must remember that, besides normal wear and tear to manuscripts and buildings, Jews suffered periodic persecutions and expulsions in Europe throughout the Middle Ages, mainly by the dominant Christian communities as well as by religious and secular rulers. Although none has survived from before the thirteenth century, there is no reason why illuminated Jewish manuscripts should not have been continuously copied and decorated with traditional biblical and midrashic illustrations.

The fact that some of these midrashic elements appear in Christian art, in the east as well as in the west, may support the assumption that Christian artists used an existing repertoire of Jewish illumination, as well as literary midrashic texts, as models for fashioning their own iconography. On folio 3 of the Golden Haggadah, bottom right, there is the non-biblical episode of Abraham being thrown into the fiery furnace by the attendants of King Nimrod. The king is seated on his throne to the right, while in the flames to the left two angels are stretching out their arms to save Abraham. This midrashic episode is recorded in several texts, stressing Abraham's staunch belief in his God.[68] According to the story, Abraham sold idols in his father's workshop, but after recognising the true Almighty, he realised how futile this was and so took a large stick and broke all the idols except the largest, in whose hands he placed the stick. When his father, Terah, came back to his workshop, Abraham explained that the largest idol had become jealous and broken all the others. 'He is an idol made of clay! How could he have done it?' exclaimed Terah. 'Let your ears hear what your mouth is uttering!' answered Abraham, 'Could these be real gods?' Not knowing how to deal with his son, Terah took him to the King of the Chaldeans, the mighty Nimrod (who is mentioned in Genesis 10:8–12 as a hunter and a king). Nimrod asked Abraham to worship his own god, fire, but Abraham suggested Nimrod should worship water, which extinguishes fire. Nimrod agreed, and Abraham then suggested worshipping rain which produces water, or the clouds which bring rain, or better still the wind which

Fig. 42. Abraham before Nimrod, and saved by God from the fire of the Chaldeans. Text illustration for the prayers for the Day of Atonement from the Leipzig *Maḥzor*. South Germany, *c.*1320. Leipzig, University Library, ms. v. 1102, vol. II, fol. 164v.

blows the clouds. When King Nimrod agreed even to this last suggestion, Abraham proposed worshipping the Almighty, the invisible God, the prime mover, whom he himself recognised. King Nimrod could not agree to this, and ordered Abraham to be cast into the fire to see whether Abraham's God would save him from Nimrod's god, fire. According to the earlier version, God sent angels to save Abraham; the later version states that it was the Almighty Himself who came down to save the only human being who recognised Him.

This whole story is a typical midrashic exposition by the rabbis to interpret Abraham's place of origin, 'Ur of the Chaldees' (Genesis 11:31), which in Hebrew also means 'the fire of the Chaldean', and to explain how Abraham was saved from the Chaldeans before going to the Land of Canaan.

This episode is similarly illustrated in the Sister to the Golden Haggadah[69], and in the Barcelona Haggadah,[70] as an interpretation of the passage in the Haggadah 'In the beginning our forefathers were idol worshippers'. Two idols illustrate the same text in the Sassoon Spanish Haggadah.[71] This midrashic story was also known to the Ashkenazi Jews of Germany, who similarly depicted angels saving Abraham from a furnace in twin Haggadoth of the early fifteenth century: the Yahudah Haggadah[72] and the Second Nuremberg Haggadah.[73] There is also one Ashkenazi representation of the scene where the hand of God, rather than the angels, saves Abraham. It appears in a south German Hebrew prayer-book of around 1300 known as the Leipzig *Maḥzor* (fig. 42).[74]

The widespread use of this midrashic scene in Hebrew illuminated manuscripts from Spain and Germany proves its popularity in Europe from the thirteenth to the fifteenth centuries. It must also have been well known to German Christian artists, who used is as an example of piety. Two manuscripts of the fourteenth century have been quoted by Joseph Gutmann[75] as representing the scene, one being a *Speculum Humanae Salvationis* and the other a *Biblia Pauperum*. They both depict Christ stretching out his arms to lift Abraham out of the fire engulfing him. This approach, similar to that of the Leipzig *Maḥzor*, may indicate a common model for all three manuscripts.

Besides the late Gothic representations, both Jewish and Christian, of this midrashic episode of Abraham being rescued from the fire of the Chaldeans, there is one Christian literary reference to its existence in the fifth century in a church in the south of Italy, now lost. St Paulinus of Nola, in the Campagna, describes in a poem the moral meanings of the paintings in his new basilica dedicated to St Felix. He states that he learns from Abraham how 'to leave my native country, once rescued from the fire of the Chaldeans'. There is no way of knowing what the painting in the basilica looked like, but the description proves that by the fifth century there was already an iconographical formula for this Jewish midrashic scene. The iconography of this, as of other midrashic episodes, must have been formulated by Jewish artists in Late Antiquity and adapted by Christian theologians and artists as a Christian martyrological scene. In most cases the Early Jewish model disappeared in the course of the Middle Ages, like its later Jewish copies. However, this special Jewish iconography appeared sporadically throughout the Middle Ages in Byzantine or western Christian illuminated manuscripts.

Two examples of such midrashic episodes in Christian manuscripts will suffice to illustrate this point. One is the temptation of Eve by the serpent in the shape of a camel, in one of the Byzantine Octateuchs of the twelfth century;[76] the other is the blind Lemech killing Cain, unwittingly aided by his grandson, whom he also kills, in the Morgan Picture Bible.[77] This midrash is depicted in many other French and English manuscripts of the Romanesque and Gothic periods, but has not survived in Hebrew manuscripts.

Midrashic Elements in the Golden Haggadah

The fact that there are many midrashic elements in Hebrew illuminated manuscripts of the Gothic period with no parallels in contemporary Latin Christian ones may indicate a continuous tradition of Jewish iconography throughout early medieval times. Many such midrashic elements appear in the illustrations of the Golden Haggadah, as can be seen from the various miniatures. Some, with parallels in Early Jewish art, have already been discussed. Other episodes in the Golden Haggadah, which have no parallels in Early Jewish art but appear in other Spanish Haggadoth or Hebrew illuminated manuscripts, show a profound knowledge of the Jewish *midrash* and the Hebrew language. Examples are the builders of the Tower of Babel killing each other (fol. 3, top left, fig. 18; *Genesis Rabbah* 38:10), since they could not understand each other after God had confused their languages; or the Israelite woman carrying a baby to be put into a brick used by the builders of the store cities in Egypt (fol. 11, top left, fig. 26; *Exodus Rabbah* 1).

During the later Middle Ages some of the old *midrashim* were rendered in a special way, indicating the complex relations between Jews and Christians at the time of their execution. One example is the ninth Plague of Darkness, as depicted in the Golden Haggadah (fol. 13, bottom left, fig. 28). The artist divided the panel horizontally into two, showing the Egyptians groping their way in darkness on top, while below, in full light, the Israelites are 'borrowing' precious objects from their houses (Exodus 11:2, 12:35). The connection between the Plague of Darkness and the Israelites 'spoiling the Egyptians' (Exodus 12:36) was made by the rabbis in a *midrash* on this verse (*Exodus Rabbah* 14:3). The contemporary element in this miniature is the fact that the Israelites are carrying a chest and gold objects which resemble church vessels, such as a chalice. None of the Christian artists or Christian theologians ever used this interpretation in any Latin illuminated manuscript.

The Creation of the Golden Haggadah

As has been shown, the iconography of the Golden Haggadah is eclectic. Many subjects were rendered in a traditional Christian manner, albeit adapted to suit a Jewish viewpoint or at least so as not to offend it. This, however, does not cover the Christian models, which were mainly full-page Gothic illuminated psalters. Other subjects reveal specifically Jewish interpretations, either in gestures or in iconographical alterations. The most obvious are those based on oral or literary *midrash*, which was the typical rabbinic exposition. Many *midrashim* were known and illustrated from Late Antiquity on, as early as the Dura Europos synagogue of the third century. Some reappear in the Haggadoth, with the same iconographic components stressed. Of these, some depictions were taken over by Christian artists, suggesting a common illustrated midrashic source for Hebrew and Latin manuscripts. Moreover, Christian midrashic representations without parallel in Hebrew manuscripts, and Jewish ones without Latin parallels, stress the existence of this common model, which must have evolved in Early Jewish art.

THE JEWS OF BARCELONA AND THE PATRONS OF THE GOLDEN HAGGADAH

The patrons who commissioned the sumptuous Spanish illuminated Haggadoth must have been Jews with not only the financial resources to pay for such luxurious manuscripts, but also the taste, discernment and interest in the visual arts necessary to enjoy them. It is profoundly unfortunate that, following the ravages of time and of deliberate destruction, so few glorious illuminated Sephardi Haggadoth have survived to bear witness to the refined taste of their patrons.

The Jewish community of Barcelona was, at the time of the creation of the Golden Haggadah, one of the most prominent and affluent in Spain. At the beginning of the fourteenth century the Kings of Aragon and the Counts of Barcelona pursued the policy of their thirteenth-century predecessors in supporting the economic and social statutes affecting the Jews.

Tradition has it that the Jewish community of Barcelona is one of the oldest in the Iberian Peninsula, dating back to Roman times or even to King Solomon's legendary expeditions to Tarshish.

Documents regarding the existence of Jews in Moslem Barcelona are extant from the end of the ninth century, when Amram Gaon, the Rabbi of Sura in Babylon, sent his version of the yearly prayer-book (*Siddur Rav Amram*) to 'the scholars of Barcelona'. As an important Mediterranean seaport, Barcelona was a Jewish commercial centre during the early Moslem period in the ninth and tenth centuries, one of the centres of the Jewish cultural Golden Age. The Jews there continued to enjoy the same economic conditions even after the Christian *Reconquista* of Spain, which was brought about in Barcelona, as in many other cities, with their help. From the middle of the eleventh century the Jews of Christian Barcelona enjoyed a preferential legal status as its citizens and the subjects of the local counts. They owned the houses in their quarter, called the *Cal* (a term derived from *kahal* = community in Hebrew), which was situated near the harbour gate of the walled city, not far from the cathedral. They also owned land for burial purposes on the 'Mountain of the Jews' (*Montjuich*), where in fact some imposing tombstones have been found.

During the twelfth and thirteenth centuries the Jews were the principal merchants in what became an Aragonese royal city. Besides their domestic and overseas trade, the Jews were artisans, prominent goldsmiths, mint-masters, physicians, astronomers and cartographers. Fluent in many languages, they were translators and diplomats acting as go-betweens for the conquered Arabic-speaking Moslem population and the conquering Catalan, Castilian, Provençal, French or Latin-speaking Christians. From the beginning of the thirteenth century the Jewish community provided lodgings for the royal household on its visits to Barcelona, and even looked after the lions in the royal menagerie.

The aristocratic Jewish families, who resided in the city for centuries, were mainly advisers, physicians, and providers of capital to the Counts of Barcelona and the Kings of Aragon. One of these families, the Benveniste, were prominent in Barcelona from the eleventh century on. One notable member, Sheshet ben Isaac ben Joseph (1131–1209, known by his Catalan name, Perfect de Pratis), a grandson of Sheshet *Ha-nasi* (= the president) of the Barcelona community, served several Counts of Barcelona and the Aragonese Kings Alfonso II and Pedro II simultaneously as physician and financier, taking an active role in the fiscal administration of the realm. As a translator into Arabic, Sheshet was a political adviser and diplomatic envoy close to the Christian nobility of the country. Like them, he was exempt from taxes, and enjoyed immunity from the jurisdiction of both the royal authorities and the Barcelona Jewish community, of which he was one of the leaders, regulating matters in the synagogue. Sheshet Benveniste was an intellectual, writing poetry and actively supporting poets; he also wrote letters on philosophical subjects in support of Maimonides in the controversy over the latter's philosophy. He was in contact with Moslem and Christian scholars, and his versatility even led him to compose some medical treatises.

Another member of the Sheshet family was the physician of James I of Aragon, Isaac ben Joseph Benveniste (died *c.*1224), a president (*nasi*) of all the Jewish communities of Aragon.

Among other prominent Jews active in Barcelona during the reign of James I was Benveniste de Porta (d. 1268), a financier to the king and a grain merchant who owned flour mills in Barcelona and became a town bailiff (*baile*). De Porta also received some exemptions from royal taxes in Catalonia and the Balearic Islands. A rich man, he too supported scholars, writers and poets in his community.

From the beginning of the thirteenth century, with the growth of the Christian merchant class and the development of other cities, the Jews were seen as rivals and their position as the most important financiers declined. In addition, as in other European countries after the Crusades, the Church's position in Spain became stronger. Pressure was put on kings and local rulers by the city merchants and the Christian mendicant orders to suspend the special statutes protecting the Jews as *Servi camerae*, namely those tied to service in the royal Fiscal Chamber, as well as their freedom to practise their religion within the community. However, kings like James I of Aragon (1213–1276) needed the financial support of the Jews, who also served as interpreters for his survey of the newly conquered Moslem lands in the south. James I urged the Jews to settle in these newly acquired lands as well as in Majorca (which he also conquered), and promised them safe conduct and communal privileges. Throughout his long reign, James I tried to protect his Jews from both the townsmen and the Christian orders, and granted them concessions to help develop their trades. The Jews' own court, the *Beit-Din*, was allowed to try any member of the community, and even to pass the death sentence, although it had to pay a fine of 1,000 *solidos* for any execution.

In 1241 James I granted the Jewish community of Barcelona a charter providing for them to be governed by a group of *ne'emanim* (= trustees), all drawn from the old, rich aristocratic families of the community. King James endorsed this charter in 1272, when the influential Rabbi Solomon ben Abraham Adret (the *RASHBA*, 1235–1310) and his sons were among the seven *ne'emanim* of the community. In his early years, before taking up his rabbinical position in Barcelona, Adret had been engaged in financial transactions with the king.

Nevertheless James I did not manage to divert all the pressure being exerted by the townspeople and the Church. In 1259 he was obliged to cancel debts to Jews; moreover, it was during his reign that the public 'Barcelona Disputation' of 1263 was forced on the Jews by pressure from the Dominican and Franciscan friars. The *Disputa* was led by the Dominicans Raymondus Martini and Raymondus de Penaforte on the Christian side, and by Rabbi Moses ben Naḥman, known as Naḥmanides, on the Jewish side. The main point at issue was whether the Christian or the Jewish religion was the true successor of the Old Testament. After four sessions King James, who presided over some of the meetings, suspended the *Disputa*, leaving it in abeyance. The most important results were the decision to erase all mentions of Jesus and Mary from the Talmud and other Jewish books; and to force the Jews to listen to Christian sermons delivered in their synagogues by friars of the mendicant orders. Naḥmanides himself left Spain, arriving in Jerusalem in 1267.

Following the example of the French king, Louis IX, the mendicant orders brought pressure to bear on the kings of Aragon to initiate a campaign to convert the Jews to Christianity by exposing the 'Jewish error' of not recognising Jesus as the Messiah. This change of climate, and the social tension within the Spanish Jewish community caused by extremes of wealth, resulted in great insecurity. This was a fertile ground for the rapid spread of the mystic ideas of the *Kabbalah*, which originated in Gerona, just north of Barcelona, and was strongly supported by Naḥmanides; the appearance of the important cabbalistic Book of the *Zohar* (= splendour) in the 1280s was the culmination of this trend. Even the rationalistic Rabbi Solomon ben Adret had to give way to pressure and in 1305 declared the study of Greek philosophy forbidden to youth under pain of excommunication.

In 1306 the Jewish community of Barcelona was augmented by about sixty rich families expelled from France by King Philippe le Bel. King James II of Aragon (1291–1327) gladly accepted them, since they constituted an important additional source of revenue, and allowed them to pursue their commercial ventures. These affluent Jews may have brought with them to Barcelona some illuminated manuscripts containing biblical illustrations with Parisian iconography and style. Such manuscripts could have been used as models by local artists to create the illustrated biblical cycle attached to the Haggadah.

King James II did not support the efforts to convert the French Jews, some of whom were permitted to return to France about ten years later, only to be expelled again in 1320, when they came back to Barcelona possibly bringing more illuminated books with them. It was only after James II's death in 1327 that a new charter was adopted for the Jews, abolishing the privileges which exempted those serving the court from paying taxes. Furthermore, parallel to the rich trustees (*ne'emanim*) of the community, a new legal body was created known as 'The Council of Thirty', which represented the less privileged members of the Jewish *aljama* (community). It was at this point that the new king yielded to the demands of the Christian merchants of Barcelona and restricted Jewish trade with Syria and Egypt.

The Black Death of 1348 hit both the Christian and the Jewish communities of Barcelona badly. Most of the *ne'emanim* and the Council of Thirty perished in the plague, yet the Jews were accused of causing it by poisoning wells. A Christian mob attacked the Jewish quarter, and despite protection from the municipality several Jews were killed and houses looted.

In spite of the deteriorating conditions, the rich Jews of Barcelona continued to prosper and to patronise the flourishing workshops producing Hebrew manuscripts, such as the sumptuous illuminated Bibles and the lavishly adorned Haggadoth. Even the decline during the second half of the fourteenth century did not bring to an end the close relations between the Jews and the kings of Aragon: Jewish goldsmiths, physicians and merchants were employed by the court, despite charges levelled at the Jews in 1367 of desecrating the Host. However, several Jewish communities did suffer as a result of these charges and some leaders were imprisoned, for example the Rabbis Isaac bar Sheshet, Nissim Gerondi and Hasdai Crescas, who were only released after payment of a large fine.

The final blow to the Barcelona community came with the persecutions of 1391. The Castilian mob, storming many towns on the way and massacring Jews in Seville and Valencia, reached Barcelona by boat, and despite the efforts of Barcelona's Christian city fathers to protect the Jews, the attack went ahead. It started on Saturday, 5 August, and lasted a week, during which the gates of the *Judería* were burnt and the castle, where the Jews had taken refuge, was stormed. The 'little people' (*populus minutus*), including dock workers and fishermen, looted houses and killed over 400 Jews, forcing the survivors to convert to Christianity. King John I of Aragon condemned twenty-six of the rioters to death and acquitted the rest. In 1393 King John attempted to restore the Jewish community in Barcelona, but without much success.

Early in the fourteenth century, however, there were several Jewish families in Barcelona who could have been patrons of sumptuous Haggadoth such as the Golden Haggadah. These Jewish merchants and court financiers were close to their fellow courtiers, who commissioned and owned illuminated psalters with full-page biblical miniatures. Admiration of these illuminated manuscripts must have led the Jewish courtiers to order similar quires of biblical illustrations from the best craftsmen they could find. Indeed, a contract dated 1335 for copying, illuminating and binding Hebrew manuscripts is known from Majorca, which formed part of the kingdom of Aragon.[78] In this contract the young man Bonim Maimo undertakes to supply several Hebrew manuscripts, to bind them, and to illuminate one of them. The contract does not specify the craftsmen to execute the work: although it is clear that the scribe, writing in Hebrew, was a Jew, the illuminator and the binder may well have been Christian. The high quality of the illuminations of the Golden Haggadah and their stylistic resemblance to royal books of the period, namely the *Usatici* of James II (fig. 33), would imply that the Haggadah was illuminated by a secular Christian craftsman. Such a Christian illuminator would have received instructions concerning the subjects and their special Jewish iconography either from the patron himself or from the scribe. In addition, the patron and the illuminator may have had other illustrated biblical manuscripts, probably brought to Barcelona by the expelled French Jews, which could have been used as models for the Golden Haggadah, and this could account for the sophisticated knowledge of Jewish midrashic elements reflected in the illustrations.

The production of the Golden Haggadah illustrates the close relations between Jews and Christians at the time. It also gives credence to the words of Rabbi Profeat Duran mentioned above, that 'it has been one of the virtues of our nation that the rich and important in every generation have always exerted an effort to produce beautiful codices'.

REFERENCES

1. Add. MS 14761, fol. 28v; Narkiss, *British*, p. 81, fig. 222.

2. I.e. praises, namely Psalms 113–118; Goldschmidt, p. 55.

3. Kaufmann, *Egyptian*.

4. Formerly Sassoon MS 514, now in The Israel Museum, MS 180/41; Narkiss, *HIM*, pl. 11.

5. Friedman.

6. Israel Museum, Jerusalem, MS 180/57; Spitzer; Narkiss, *HIM*, pl. 28.

7. Israel Museum, MS 180/50, Narkiss, 'Yahudah'.

8. Jerusalem, Schocken Library, MS 24087; Müller & Schlosser, pp. 125–170, Taf. XVI–XXVI; Narkiss, *HIM*, pls. 40, 41; Narkiss & Sed, II/2, 3.

9. Add. MS 14761, Narkiss, *HIM*, pl. 12; Narkiss, *British*, No. 13.

10. British Library, Add. MS 27210; Narkiss, *Golden*; Narkiss, *HIM*, pl. 8; Narkiss, *British*, I, pp. 58–66, figs. 123–154.

11. Sarajevo, National Museum; see Roth; Müller & Schlosser.

12. Library of Congress, MS Heb. I; Narkiss, *HIM*, pl. 50; Narkiss, 'Washington'.

13. Margoliouth, II, No. 607; Narkiss, *Golden*, p. 79; Narkiss, *British*, I, No. 11.

14. Goldschmidt, pp. 5–13, 63–68.

15. Narkiss, *Golden*, pp. 11–16.

16. Goldschmidt, pp. 98–103.

17. Narkiss, *Golden*, pp. 5–6.

18. Luzzatto.

19. Narkiss, *Golden*, pp. 1–2, note 1.

20. Narkiss, *Golden*, pp. 1–2, notes 4–9.

21. Popper, pp. 78–79; Narkiss, *Golden*, pp. 3–4, note 12.

22. Popper, pp. 82, 100–101, 123; Narkiss, *Golden*, p. 4, notes 13, 15, 16.

23. Babylonian Talmud, *Pesaḥim* 37a; Jerusalem Talmud, *Pesaḥim* II, 4.

24. Now Israel Museum, MS 180/41, pp. 16–17; Sassoon, I, p. 303; Narkiss, *Golden*, pp. 20–21.

25. Add. MS 14761, fol. 61; Narkiss, *HIM*, pl. 12.

26. Berlin, Staatsbibliothek, Preussischer Kulturbesitz, Ham. 288; Narkiss, *HIM*, pl. 7.

27. Lisbon, National Library, MS Ill. 72; Narkiss, *HIM*, pl. 6, fig. 2.

28. Cambridge, University Library, MS N-S. 324, see Narkiss, *HIM* in Hebrew, p. 28, fig. 17.

29. Porcher, pls. XLVI–LII.

30. Cockerell & James; Plummer.

31. Millar, *Somme*; Millar, *Honoré*.

32. Porcher, pl. XLVIII.

33. Salmi, figs. 17, 19, 46, 50, pl. VI.

34. Salmi, figs. 21, 25, 27, 35, 47, pls. X, XV, XX, XXXI.

35. Salmi, pp. 18–20, 34–36, figs. 16–19, 45, pl. XXVI.

36. Bunim, pp. 131–143, figs. 49–52.

37. White.

38. MS 83, MQ 165, see Kaufmann; for fol. 72v, see Avril, p. 46.

39. Bibliothèque Royale, MS 9169, Domínguez-Bordona, figs. 182, 183; Avril, pp. 67-69.

40. Bibliothèque Nationale, MS lat. 8846, Domínguez-Bordona, p. 153, figs. 187, 188, pl. V; Avril, p. 70.

41. Meiss.

42. Bibliothèque Nationale, MS lat. 4670A; Domínguez-Bordona, pp. 106, 143, figs. 172–174; Narkiss, *Golden*, pp. 38, 39, 41 note 30, figs. 7–10; Avril, *Spanish*, No. 105, fol. 67; Avril, p. 48.

43. Narkiss, *Golden*, p. 39.

44. Meiss.

45. Roth, *Sarajevo*.

46. Narkiss, *Golden*, p. 79.

47. Biblioteca Palatina, MS 2411.

48. Cod. 2761.

49. Or. MS 2737; Narkiss, *British*, No. 9.

50. New York, Pierpont Morgan Library, MS M. 638; Plummer, fol. 7v, p. 52.

51. Plummer, fol. 9v, p. 28.

52. Paris, Bibliothèque Nationale, MS lat. 10525, fol. 31v; Thomas, pl. 31.

53. Amiens, Bibliothèque Municipale, MS lat. 108, fol. 43; Bucher, pl. 107.

54. Harburg, Öttingen-Wallerstein Collection, MS I.2, fol. 53; Bucher, p. 215.

55. Fol. 19v; Thomas, pl. 29.

56. *Targum Pseudo-Jonathan* to Exodus 2:1–6; Sed, *Bible*, p. 99; Shalev.

57. Library of the Hungarian Academy of Sciences, Budapest, MS A 422, fol. 10; Sed, *Kaufmann*.

58. *Book of Jubilees* 47:5; Josephus, *Jewish Antiquities* II.4.223.

59. Harburg, Prince Öttingen-Wallerstein Collection, MS I.2, fol. 49; Bucher, pl. 99.

60. New York, Public Library, Spencer Collection MS 22, fol. 41v; Bucher, vol. I, p. 215, fig. 31a.

61. Kraeling, pl. LXVIII; Goodenough, vol. IX, pp. 197ff., vol. XI, pl. IX.

62. Kraeling, pl. LIII; Goodenough, vol. X, pp. 105ff., vol. XI, pl. XIV, left part.

63. Manchester, MS Heb. 6, fol. 19; Narkiss, *British*, No. 15, p. 90; Loewe.

64. British Library, Or. MS 1404, fol. 7v; Narkiss, *British*, No. 16, pp. 96–97, fig. 294.

65. fol. 28; Sed, *Bible*, p. 106, fig. 120.

66. *Pirkei d'Rabbi Eli'ezer*, ch. 43; Narkiss, *Pharaoh*.

67. Harburg, MS I.2, fol. 57v; Bucher, pl. 118.

68. *Midrash Genesis Rabbah* 38:13; Babylonian Talmud, *Pesaḥim* 118a; *Tana d'vei Eliyahu* 6.

69. British Library, Or. MS 2884, fol. 3; Narkiss, *British*, No. 12, fig. 158.

70. British Library, Add. MS 14761, fol. 35v; Narkiss, *British*, No. 13, fig. 230.

71. Israel Museum, MS 180/41, p. 61; Narkiss, *HIM*, pl. 11; Narkiss, *Golden*, fig. 34.

72. Israel Museum, MS 180/50, fol. 29v; Narkiss, *Yahudah*; Narkiss, *HIM*, pl. 41; Narkiss & Sed, vol. 2, No. 3.

73. Schocken Library, MS 24087, fol. 30v; Narkiss, *HIM*, pl. 40; Narkiss & Sed, vol. 2, No. 2; Sed, *Bible*, p. 32, fig. 22.

74. Leipzig, University Library, MS V. 1102, vol. II, fol. 164v; Narkiss, *Lipsiae*; Gutmann, *Manuscript*, pl. 25.

75. *Abraham*.

76. Weitzmann.

77. fol. 2r; Plummer, p. 30.

78. Hillgarth & Narkiss.

BIBLIOGRAPHY

Ameisenowa
Ameisenowa, Z., 'Some neglected representations of the Harmony of the Universe', *Essays in honour of Hans Tieze 1880–1954 (Gazette des Beaux-Arts, 1950–58)*, Paris, 1958, pp. 350 ff.

Avril
Avril, F., *L'enluminure à l'époque gotique 1200–1240*, Paris, 1995.

Avril, *Spanish*
Avril, F., Aniel, J.-P., Mentré, M., Saulnier, A., and Zaluksa, Y., *Manuscrits enluminés de la Péninsule Ibérique*, Paris, 1983.

Bohigas
Bohigas, P., *La Ilustración y la decoración del libro manuscrito en Cataluña*, I–II, Barcelona, 1965.

Bucher
Bucher, F., *The Pamplona Bibles*, New Haven, 1970.

Bunim
Bunim-Schild, M., *Space in Medieval Painting and the Forerunners of Perspective*, New York, 1940.

Cockerell & James
Cockerell, S.C., and James, M.R., *A Book of Old Testament Illustrations of the Middle of the Thirteenth Century*, Cambridge, 1927.

Domínguez-Bordona
Domínguez-Bordona, J., 'Miniatura', *Ars Hispaniae*, 18, Madrid, 1962, pp. 17–242.

Friedman
Friedman, M., 'The Four Sons of the Haggadah and the Ages of Man', *Journal of Jewish Art*, 11 (1985), pp. 16–40.

Goldschmidt
Goldschmidt, E.D., *The Passover Haggadah, its Sources and History* (in Hebrew), Jerusalem, 1960.

Goodenough
Goodenough, E.R., *Dura Europos Synagogue*, in *Jewish Symbols in the Greco-Roman Period*, vols. 9–11, Princeton, 1964.

Gutmann, *Abraham*
Gutmann, J., 'Abraham in the Fire of the Chaldeans: A Jewish Legend in Jewish, Christian and Islamic Art', *Frühmittelalterliche Studien*, 7 (1973), pp. 342–352.

Gutmann, *Antiquity*
Gutmann, J., 'The Illustrated Jewish Manuscripts in Antiquity – The Present State of the Question', *Gesta*, 5 (1966), pp. 39–44.

Gutmann, *Haggadah*
Gutmann, J., 'The Illuminated Medieval Haggadah: Investigations and Research Problems', *Studies in Bibliography and Booklore*, VII (1965), pp. 3–25.

Gutmann, *Manuscript*
Gutmann, J., *Hebrew Manuscript Painting*, New York, 1978.

Gutmann, *Motif*
Gutmann, J., 'The Haggadic Motif in Jewish Iconography', *Eretz Israel*, 6 (1960), pp. 16-22.

Hillgarth & Narkiss
Hillgarth, J., and Narkiss, B., 'A list of Hebrew Books (1330) and a Contract to Illuminate Manuscripts (1335) from Majorca', *Revue des Etudes Juives*, CXX (1961), pp. 297–320.

Kaufmann
Kaufmann, C.M., 'Vidal Major', *Aachener Kunstblätter*, 29 (1964), pp. 109–138.

Kaufmann, *Egyptian*
Kaufmann, D., 'Notes on the Egyptian Fragments of the Haggadah', *Jewish Quarterly Review*, 10 (1898), pp. 380 ff.

Kraeling, *Dura*
Kraeling, C.H., et al., *The Synagogue, The Excavations at Dura-Europos*, Final Report, III, part I, New Haven, 1956.

Loewe
Loewe, R., *The Rylands Haggadah*, London, 1988.

Luzzatto
Luzzatto, S.D., *Catalogue de la bibliothèque de littérature hébraïque et orientale de feu M. Joseph Almanzi*, Padua, 1864.

Margoliouth
Margoliouth, G., *The Catalogue of the Hebrew and Samaritan Manuscripts in the British Museum*, London, 1905.

Meiss
Meiss, M., 'Italian Style in Catalonia and a fourteenth-century Catalan Workshop', *Journal of the Walters Art Gallery*, 4 (1941), pp. 45–87.

Metzger, *Haggadah*
Metzger, M., *La Haggada Enluminée*, Leiden, 1973.

Millar, *Honoré*
Millar, E.G., *The Parisian Miniaturist Honoré*, London, 1959.

Millar, *Somme*
Millar, E.G., *An Illuminated Manuscript of La Somme le Roy*, Oxford, 1953. (Now British Library Add. MS 54180).

Müller & Schlosser
Müller, D.H., Schlosser, J. von, and Kaufmann, D., *Die Haggadah von Sarajevo*, Vienna, 1898.

Narkiss, *British*
Narkiss, B., *Hebrew Illuminated Manuscripts in the British Isles. A Catalogue Raisonné*, vol.I, *The Spanish and Portuguese Manuscripts*, Jerusalem & Oxford, 1982.

Narkiss, *Golden*
Narkiss, B., *The Golden Haggadah. A fourteenth-century illuminated Hebrew manuscript in the British Museum*, Introduction to the Facsimile Edition, London, 1970.

Narkiss, *HIM*
Narkiss, B., *Hebrew Illuminated Manuscripts*, Jerusalem and New York, 1969 (in Hebrew 1984).

Narkiss, *Lipsiae*
Narkiss, B., 'Introduction to the Mahzor Lipsiae', in E.Katz (ed.), *Machsor Lipsiae*, Facsimile and Introduction, Leipzig, 1964.

Narkiss, *Pharaoh*
Narkiss, B., 'Pharaoh is Dead and Living at the Gates of Hell', *Journal of Jewish Art*, 10 (1984), pp.6–13.

Narkiss, *Washington*
Narkiss, B., 'The Style and Iconography of the Washington Haggadah', in *Introduction to the Facsimile of the Washington Haggadah*, Washington, 1990.

Narkiss & Sed
Narkiss, B., and Sed-Rajna, G., *Index of Jewish Art, Iconographical Index of Hebrew Illuminated Manuscripts*, Jerusalem and Paris, vol.1, 1976; vol.2, 1981; vol.3, 1983; vol.4, 1990; vol.5, 1994; vol.6, 1996.

Narkiss, *Yahudah*
Narkiss, M., 'The Yahudah Haggadah', *The Jerusalem Post*, 6th April 1955.

Plummer
Plummer, J., and Cockerell, S.C., *Old Testament Miniatures*, New York, 1969.

Popper
Popper, W., *The Censorship of Hebrew Books*, New York, 1899.

Porcher
Porcher, J., *French Miniatures*, Paris, 1960.

Roth, *Haggadah*
Roth, C., *The Haggadah: a New Edition with an English Translation*, London, 1934.

Roth, *Sarajevo*
Roth, C., *The Sarajevo Haggadah*, Belgrade, 1963.

Salmi
Salmi, M., *Italian Miniatures*, London, 1957.

Sassoon
Sassoon, D.S., *Ohel David. Descriptive Catalogue of the Hebrew and Samaritan Manuscripts in the Sassoon Library, London*, vols. I, II, Oxford, 1932.

Sed, *Bible*
Sed-Rajna, G., *The Hebrew Bible in Medieval Illuminated Manuscripts*, New York, 1987.

Sed, *Kaufmann*
Sed-Rajna, G., *The Kaufmann Haggadah, Introduction to the Facsimile*, Budapest, 1990.

Shalev
Shalev-Eini, S., 'The Rebirth of Pharaoh's Daughter in Finding Moses', *Rimonim*, 5 (1996).

Spitzer
Spitzer, M. (ed.), with E.D.Goldschmidt, H.L.C.Jaffe, B.Narkiss and M.Shapiro, *The Birds' Head Haggadah*, Facsimile Edition and an Introduction, Jerusalem, 1967.

Stein
Stein, S., 'The Influence of Symposia Literature on the Literary Form of the Pesach Haggadah', *Journal of Jewish Studies*, VIII (1957), pp.13–44.

Thomas
Thomas, M., *Psautier de S.Louis*, I–II, Graz, 1970.

Weitzmann
Weitzmann, K., 'The Illustration of the Septuagint', *Studies in Classical and Byzantine Manuscript Illumination*, Chicago and London, 1971, pp.45–75.

White
White, J., *The Birth and Rebirth of Pictorial Space*, London, 1957, p.82.